FROM HOPE TO LIBERATION

FROM HOPE
TO LIBERATION

TOWARDS A NEW
MARXIST-CHRISTIAN DIALOGUE

edited by NICHOLAS PIEDISCALZI
ROBERT G. THOBABEN

with contributions by HERBERT APTHEKER
SHEPHERD BLISS
THOMAS W. OGLETREE

FORTRESS PRESS   Philadelphia

For our progeny

BOB, TOM AND CORDT THOBABEN
and
SHELL, LISA AND NICKY PIEDISCALZI

CONTENTS

PREFACE

This book is intended as an introduction to the Marxist-Christian dialogue for undergraduate students and lay persons. An introduction by Robert Thobaben describes and assesses the origins and nature of the dialogue in the Western world and the new encounter arising in the Third World. Two essays derive from an actual dialogue conducted at Wright State University by Herbert Aptheker and Thomas Ogletree. These two presentations on the topic "What May Man Really Hope For?" epitomize the type of dialogue conducted in the West. They are followed by the responses of Aptheker and Ogletree to each other, some questions addressed to both men by Wright State University students and faculty, and the replies of the two speakers. Shepherd Bliss's essay examines the Aptheker-Ogletree dialogue from the perspective of an active participant in the Third World dialogue. Bliss points out what he considers to be its weaknesses and describes and affirms the new dialogue emerging in the Third World. A concluding essay by Nicholas Piediscalzi describes the present status and prospects of the dialogue.

This book differs from others on the dialogue in that it is the first systematic approach to the Marxist-Christian encounter that is directed to lay persons and undergraduate students. It is also unique in that it includes a critique from the Third World perspective directly related to the essays which precede it. The introductory and concluding essays introduce students and lay persons to the major issues and problems in the dialogue. The book also points out the plateau which has been reached in the Western encounter and suggests the way in which the Third World dialogue may be able to lead the Western encounter beyond its present resting place.

The idea of conducting a Marxist-Christian dialogue and of writing this book grew out of a team-taught, interdisciplinary course that the editors conducted at Wright State University. Entitled "The Marxist-Christian Dialogue," its basic assumption, as with all other interdisciplinary courses taught at Wright State, was that contemporary higher education in the United States is overspecialized and fragmented and that attempts must be made to reintegrate artificially separated and competing academic disciplines.

In organizing the dialogue and preparing the book a number of individuals and groups gave us valuable assistance. We want to thank Dean Eugene B. Cantelupe and the faculty committee administering the Liberal Arts College Research Fund for providing encouragement and funds. Our gratitude goes also to the University Center Board, the Student Senate and the Liberal Arts Lecture Series Committee for supplying an important part of the funds necessary for the dialogue. To Mary Soter, Edith Davidson, Vicki Bruns and Kathy Knape we wish to express our thanks for their excellent work in transcribing the original pages and in typing the various drafts which preceded publication.

We are also indebted to Verniece Osborne, Media Equipment Distribution Supervisor, and her staff for their courteous and prompt service. In addition, we wish to express our thanks to Alberta Stewart and Diane Johnson for organizing and acting as hostesses at the dinner preceding the dialogue.

A special expression of appreciation is due to Dr. Herbert Neve of the Wright State University Department of Religion. In addition to reading and criticizing constructively the entire manuscript, he provided helpful bibliographies and assisted the editors in establishing contacts and consultations with leaders in Europe.

Though many have helped us, the editors and contributors alone are responsible for what is said in the book.

N.P.
R.G.T.

CONTRIBUTORS AND EDITORS

Herbert Aptheker, a historian by profession, is the National Director of the American Institute for Marxist Studies (New York City). A voluminous and prolific writer, Dr. Aptheker has contributed several articles and two books, to the Marxist-Christian dialogue, *Marxism and Christianity* and *The Urgency of the Marxist-Christian Dialogue.*

Shepherd Bliss, a United Methodist minister, is director of the Latin American Project at the Cambridge-Goddard Graduate School for Social Change. His articles on Latin American Christianity and education have appeared in *Christian Century, Christianity and Crisis,* and *American Report.*

Thomas W. Ogletree is Associate Professor of Theological Ethics at Vanderbilt University's Divinity School. The author of several books and articles, Professor Ogletree has been a leader in the American Marxist-Christian dialogue. He edited and contributed an introductory essay to the book *Openings for Marxist-Christian Dialogue,* which has also been translated into Japanese.

Nicholas Piediscalzi is Professor and Chairman of the Department of Religion at Wright State University (Dayton, Ohio). He also serves as co-director of the Public Education Religion Studies Center. Professor Piediscalzi received a B.A. from Grinnell College, B.D. from Yale University Divinity School, and Ph.D. from Boston University. He also studied as a special student under Erik H. Erikson at Harvard University. He is co-editor of the book *Contemporary Religion and Social Responsibility* and the author of several articles.

Robert G. Thobaben, Associate Professor in the Department of Political Science at Wright State University, is a native of Cleveland, Ohio. He received a B.S.C. from Ohio University, an M.A. from Miami University and a Ph.D. from the University of Cincinnati. During the 1972–73 academic year he studied at the Goethe Institute in Germany and did research on the Marxist-Christian Dialogue at Cambridge University in England.

INTRODUCTION

ROBERT G. THOBABEN

The New Creative Tension

Origin. There is a new creative tension in the dialogue between Marxists and Christians. This dynamic stress does not originate in the organized and institutionalized Communist parties and Christian churches of the Western world. The behavior of the people who make up these constituencies, their structures of decision-making, their bureaucracies and their institutions of communication and evaluation are still highly predictable. With few exceptions they continue to recite their worn wisdom. These two groups neither view realistically nor respond adequately to the monumental changes in technology, social structure and political economy that have occurred since the last days of World War II. These changes include cybernetics, automation, exploration of space, penetration of the atom, new roles for women, young people and non-whites, bureaucratic proliferation and the decolonization of the Third World.[1] Old theories and new environmental conditions simply cannot continue to co-exist.

The point here is not to castigate the large number of Communists and Christians who have held rigid, fundamentalist interpretations, but rather to note the danger of such a practice as a debilitating virus—present or incipient in all belief systems. *Any* ideology

1

or theology that is hesitant to test its "Truths" or probe its "Realities" becomes deterministic in time—be it Marxism, Christianity, Capitalism, Judaism or Democracy—and this determinism works to create unbridgeable gaps and antagonisms between its advocates and adherents to other belief systems. When such dogmatism prevails, political power, economic control and ecclesiastical authority become the chief values of the group, not human well-being in history.

Therefore, if it is true that a genuine Christianity implies the need for criticism and reform, and if it is true that authentic Marxism demands constant critique, then questions and creative action, not answers and obedience, must characterize the thought and action of the believers. Such has not been the case to date in most instances.

The new creative tension does not originate within the organized church and party, but neither does it emerge from the old Marxist-Christian dialogue that has been conducted in the First and Second World countries for the past decade. De-Stalinization and Papal overtures in the late 1950's and early 1960's were the twin catalysts of the first dialogues between Marxists and Christians. Some of these initial encounters were even clandestine because the risks and opportunities of dialogue simply were not clear enough to either the established leaders or the intellectuals involved.[2] But as time and experience demonstrated to both sides that many of their fears were unfounded, the dialogue was gradually conducted more openly throughout Western and Eastern Europe and in Canada. Important as this first phase of the Marxist-Christian dialogue was, the argument here is that the new vitality in this dialogue does not flow from this group of dialogists.

Paradoxically, the new creative tension is not founded on differences between Marxists and Christians at all. On the contrary, it is founded on the tension between two different groups of Marxists and Christians—one group participating in the dialogue in the First and Second World nations and a second group operating in the Third World countries. Today there are two quite separate and distinct Marxist-Christian dialogues going on in the world.

Similarities and Differences. In some ways these parallel encounters are similar and in some ways they are different. The similarities are to be found in the common values and beliefs of the participants. First, both groups of dialogists recognize the excessive idealism of the so-called unbridgeable gulf that allegedly separates Marxists and Christians in their thought and social action. Second, both reject a deterministic interpretation of Marxist and Christian thought as being completely antithetical to the central doctrines of these two thought systems. Third, both reject centralized and authoritarian practices within the party and church. Fourth, both question seriously the cult of nationalism that has been grafted onto Marxism and Christianity in all three worlds. Fifth, both reject class society, whether the old aristocratic class or the new élite class. Sixth, both seem to be trying to recapture the magnificent moral vision lost or forgotten in the political struggles of their respective groups. Finally, both embrace the values of humanism and deplore the level of alienation present in all social systems.[3]

3

Though these uniformities unite the two groups of dialogists, it is their differences that generate the developmental and progressive element with which we are concerned here. These differences are found in the physical and cultural realities present in the First and Second Worlds vis-à-vis those in the Third World. For example, the nations in which these parallel dialogues occur are completely different in a socio-economic sense; the nations of the First and Second Worlds are developed, while those of the Third World remain underdeveloped. The central problem of the overwhelming number of people is different—psychological estrangement in the First and Second Worlds, physical existence in the Third World. The number and quality of people varies dramatically: in the First and Second Worlds one sees a mangeable number of people, who are literate, physically healthy, with some measure of social mobility; while in the Third World one still notes catastrophic population growth coupled with illiterate, ill-fed, ill-housed people—people with almost no chance to change their social relationships. Finally, the experience of the inhabitants with respect to the phenomena of colonialism, imperialism and racism is different; exploiting, white superiors compose the developed world, while exploited, nonwhite inferiors make up the underdeveloped world. To generalize, the milieus in which the two dialogues occur today are so dramatically different that they are literally and figuratively poles apart. Rich versus poor, north versus south, developed versus underdeveloped—however one chooses to describe the world, the differences are there. And it is these differences that give rise to the gap between the two Marxist-Christian dialogues, a gap that in process of being established and bridged has revitalized the world wide encounter. This is the significance of the addition of the new Marxist-Christian dialogue to the old encounter, and each without the other is idealistic, partial and distorted.

Genesis of the Dialogue. No precise date can be established as a specific first meeting of participants in the Marxist-Christian dialogue. But some quiet conversations between Christian theologians and Communist theorists in Eastern Europe in the early 1960's and two encyclicals of Pope John XXIII, *Mater et Magistra* in 1961 and *Pacem in Terris* in 1963, were important preconditions for the nascent dialogue.[4] Khrushchev's "watershed" speech to the Twentieth Party Congress in 1956, denouncing Stalinist excesses,[5] and the redefinition of doctrine at this same assembly also pointed the way to the possibility of new, harmonious relationships between formerly hostile groups.[6] Marxists such as Maurice Thorez of France, Dr. Erika Kadlecova of Czechoslovakia, Palmiro Togliatti of Italy, Roger Garaudy of France, Leszek Kolakowski of Poland, Gajo Petrovich of Yugoslavia and Herbert Aptheker of the United States have contributed to the opening and development of the dialogue, as did the Second Vatican Council, the Geneva Conference on Church and Society and such theologians as Rosemary Ruether, J. M. Lochmann, Jürgen Moltmann, Harvey Cox, Charles C. West and Thomas Ogletree. This period of the old discourse was almost exclusively dominated by participants from the First and Second Worlds, and their meetings and assemblies were invariably held in those communities.

Procedural and theoretical questions first occupied the attention of these early dialogists. In the area of philosophy there were many thoughtful and developmental essays on metaphysics, epistemological questions, ethics and aesthetics. What is basic and essential in both Marxism and Christianity was clarified, and what elements of each faith system should be revised and developed were argued out. Social and religious categories were then examined, including such concepts as immanence, transcendence, love, subjectivity and eschatology, along with ideas about man, society, human freedom and responsibility, history and historical change.[7]

The second stage of the dialogue began later in the Third World countries, and the questions to which these participants address themselves are quite different. Although it is difficult to set a precise date for the establishment of this new, second dialogue, certainly the establishment of a Communist political system in Cuba in 1959, coupled with the charisma of Fidel Castro, contributed to the dialogue in Latin America. As Reverend James Conway stated on the *Today* television show, June 6, 1972, Castro had a priest with him in the hills prior to the actual seizure of power, he was educated by Catholic priests as a youth and he even accepted a Bible from a church leader on his extended visit to Chile.

One of the most recent examples of the existence of the dialogue in the Third World is associated with the election of Salvador Allende as President of Chile in 1970. The democratic election, inauguration and administration of an avowed Marxist in an underdeveloped Latin American nation created the perfect milieu for the new second stage in the dialogue. During the spring of 1972 over 400 Christians from 25 countries met in Santiago, Chile, calling themselves "Christians for Socialism" and all espousing Marxist doctrines in the area of social analysis. They considered themselves good Christians and they saw no irreconcilable contradictions between the two mentalities. To them Marxism was an ethical challenge to do something about the miserable social conditions of the millions of people of Latin America. Marxism seemed to them to offer particularly acute theoretical instruments of social analysis. Thus they used these and simply did not address themselves to the philosophical questions. To these Christians, Marxism had to be distinguished from Stalinism, just as real Christian faith involved more than the individual experience of church on Sunday since it also meant that Christians and Christianity must be active and effective in the process of social change.[8]

Now practical questions have taken their proper place in the dialogue. These questions are associated with the necessities of life—food, clothing, shelter, fuel and medical care. These Third World Marxists appear to be particularly determined to give meaning to the epitaph on Marx's tombstone, the eleventh thesis on Feuerbach, "The philosophers have only interpreted the world in various ways; the point, however, is to change it."[9] These Christians from the poor countries understand their theology in terms of the intimate connection between faith and work as suggested in Jesus' charge to all the faithful, "Wherefore by their fruits ye shall know them,"[10] and in the general epistle of James 1:22–23, "But be ye doers of the word, and not hearers only, deceiving your ownselves. For if any be a hearer of the word, and not a doer, he is like unto a man beholding his natural face in a glass."[11]

The addition of a Third World dimension to the Marxist-Christian encounter that had been taking place for a decade in the First and Second World countries has energized the dialogue. A new dialectical relationship between the two dialogues has been established. Now theory can be tested. Now action can be rationally oriented. Now real progress can occur. Creative human activity is the new force flowering in the dialogue today —there is "movement in the body." Prior to the Latin American experience, the animation in the encounter was mainly cerebral; today, the body as well as the mind is beginning to stir. Practice and good works have joined forces with theory and authentic faith to couple direct political action with innovative thought. In brief, then, the new creative tension in the Marxist-Christian dialogue is a consequence of the addition of a second, practice-oriented discourse in the Third World countries.

The Second Stage of Development

What, precisely, is novel and unique in this new, worldwide encounter? Simply, what's new in the new Marxist-Christian dialogue? The argument advanced here is that virtually everything is new, from the relationships of the participants to the nature and form of the dialogue itself.

New Relationships. Without being too jargonistic, the relationship of the participants in the new Marxist-Christian dialogue is best thought of horizontally as opposed to vertically. Although there are many different ways that one can think about the links that unite people into a group, one of the most widespread techniques is to talk about people who embrace the same ideology. Thus we speak about Communists, Anarchists, Jews, Christians, Capitalists or Socialists. In so doing, we relate people to one another by what they believe, by the system of thought that orients their lives. This is a vertical-structural definition of human association.

An alternate way to think about human relationships is to describe people in terms of their activity. When we do this, we talk about students, professors, radical young people, judges and workers. Here people are united not by what they think so much as by what they are doing. This is a horizontal-functional description of human association.

The relationship of the dialogists in the Third World is basically horizontal and functional. The Marxists and Christians involved here are basically related by what they do and not what they believe. This functional relationship cuts across ideologies as it acts to bind them together. So concerned are they with the material job at hand, *i.e.*, the satisfaction of the necessities of life for *all* the people, that they have been able to cut through the ideological cocoons that surround them. The impor-

9

tance of doing political work—of doing "good political work"[12] as defined above—is simply more important to them than the analysis of philosophical categories. There is no doubt that Marxists and Christians still have significant philosophical differences in the area of metaphysics, or ontology as the Marxists prefer. It is true that they have differences on the origin and nature of man as well as on the nature and role of religion. Nevertheless, one can identify people today who call themselves Marxist Christians or Christian Marxists. The problems of human existence have simply persuaded these people that they will have to forego the joys of symmetry and theoretical consistency if they hope to save the lives of living human individuals.

The relationship of the participants in the old Marxist-Christian dialogue is most usefully viewed as vertical and structural. Their association is founded on a similar intellectual attitude toward each other and toward their respective thought systems. This group of dialogists in the First and Second Worlds is linked by a common predisposition with respect to intellectual inquiry. This is certainly an important social cement, but their membership in specific ideological groups is still quite clear. The participants here still see themselves, their fellow discussants, the world and their relationships in that world from the security of their individual mentalities. There are few Marxist Christians here.

New Stages and Features. The old Marxist-Christian dialogue has four levels of development (1961 to 1974). The first stage was concerned with questions of procedure. These "ground rules" of the dialogue involved questions on who should participate, the nature of a genuine dialogue, the proper form of the encounter and what constitutes the right attitude for participants.[13] The second stage was the period of justification. Here the participants were interested in questions of why the dialogue was urgent and right and what the significance of the encounter really was.[14] The third stage of the old polemic, perhaps the most intellectually fascinating stage to date, attempts to probe the parameters of the old theoretical realities. Roger Garaudy's discussion of dialectics is one of the best examples of this probing. Garaudy argues that dialectics, the Marxist theory of knowledge, should be constructed on the notion of model. He holds that this notion sensitizes one to forward movement and reference to an exterior reality and that it tends to de-dogmatize the category.[15] Jürgen Moltmann criticizes the popular Christian conception of freedom and argues that Jesus' life and crucifixion demonstrates that Christian freedom can no longer be associated with the struggle for power. In the future it must be related to love and solidarity with the powerless.[16]

Rosemary Ruether in her book *The Radical Kingdom* posits a theology of revolution. She argues that Christians must not forget their revolutionary traditions and that it is urgent that the relationship between Christian practice and this form of social change be re-established.[17] Adam Schaff, a Marxist philosopher in Poland, constructs an entirely new concept of the human individual. He asserts that living man is the starting point and central value of socialism and always has been, and he quotes at length from Marx to document his assertions. Traditional Communist constructions defining the relationship of the individual and society are superficial and distorted according to Schaff, and in the new construction, the correct balance between the two is re-established.[18] These are just a few of the examples of the excellent work of the dialogists at this third stage of the old encounter.

The fourth period of the dialogue is involved with new categories that Marxists and Christians have not yet fully explored. These include questions concerning death, the persistence of alienation, the correspondence or incongruity of love and violent struggle and the possibility of the end of ideology and theology.

The new Marxist-Christian dialogue has only two internal levels of development (1965–1974). These stages of change are best described by the action of the participants. Initially, the activist level of the encounter was conducted by individuals or small groups —one or a few people speaking and acting. Leszek Kolakowski's essay "What Socialism is Not" and the anomic action that followed is one instance.[19] The behavior of Camilo Torres, the priest turned revolutionary, is another. Here a Colombian priest set aside clerical privilege and dedicated himself completely to the process of revolution in a guerrilla band.[20]

But beginning in July, 1966, large group action began to appear. The activity of the radical theologians and lay people in Geneva at the World Council of Churches meeting on Church and Society that year, the activities of many young people associated with the Centro de Estudios Sobre Tenencia during the early 1970's, the work of many young priests in Latin America and the assembly of Christians for Socialism in 1972

—all testify to the vitality of the people at this level of the encounter. What is particularly striking here is that not only are new issues being ventilated but new practices are emerging.

New Tactics and Strategy. The behavior and attitudes of the people involved in the old Marxist-Christian dialogue reflect a tactical agreement on behavior but maintain a strategic disagreement in their psychological and intellectual posture. Behavior is polite, almost genteel. Deference to one another in public forum and private communications is the rule. However, their psychological and intellectual commitments still make them best understood in terms of an ideological or theological allegiance. In the new dialogue just the reverse is true. This group disagrees on a score of behavior problems associated with how one should best approach the resolution of a problem—strife, protest, anomic action or petition. But they fundamentally agree intellectually and psychologically on where they are going. Principle gives way to planning, and the best possible solution gives way to the most probable one. Land tenure, milk for children, housing and the control of political and economic institutions demand their attention. Rational change in light of experience toward an authentic socialist community is their goal.

Other New Distinctions. The origin and location of the two dialogues are different. The old dialogue began in the developed nations years before its new counterpart got started in the underdeveloped countries. The form of the old encounter reflects traditional academia, *i.e.*, symposiums, letters, seminars, books of essays and forums of various kinds. The form of the new dialogue is represented by working groups and program-directed political activity. The objects of concern among the participants in the developed nations—the people to whom the dialogue is directly and objectively directed —are the political and intellectual elites in the Western world. The poor nation dialogists do just the opposite; their direct concern is hungry human beings. Even the legal status of the two groups reveals differences; the first is generally permitted, the second at times not even tolerated.

The New Marxist-Christian Dialogue: Implications and Possibilities

There are many fascinating theoretical and social implications and possibilities generated by the new Marxist-Christian dialogue. However, the real significance of these new theoretical developments and practical opportunities lies not so much in quantity as it does in quality. Historical categories, as opposed to extra-historical constructions, appear to be the major beneficiary. Four of these warrant comment.

On the Dialogue Itself. The opportunity to test theory in an empirical context is always the best foundation upon which any credible hypothesis can be constructed, evaluated, revised and developed, particularly social theory. This possibility now exists. The activities in countries such as Yugoslavia and Chile, coupled with the overtures being made in China, Tanzania, Cuba, Mexico and India, have revitalized the meetings of Marxists and Christians that were becoming static and lifeless. The old and new dialogues give life to each other in much the same way that free and open criticism of policy, process and people invigorates any truly democratic association, whether religious, social, economic or political.

The scope of the dialogue is expanding, becoming worldwide rather than regional. The new encounter in the Third World communities creates the condition for a truly ecumenical dialogue at some future time. Perhaps some day even a congress or conference of representatives from different parts of the world might deal with fundamental questions such as "Love and the Class Struggle." What do these categories mean to Marx ists and Christians in different circumstances? To what extent are these really mutually exclusive categories? What different kinds of actions are implied for Marxists and Christians today, here, now, in all Three Worlds? These categories form the foundation of each faith system's historical analysis, but little inquiry has been done to date to understand what they mean in 1974.

Hundreds of new participants are and will be actively involved in the Marxist-Christian dialogue in all three worlds. What was formerly a relatively closed fraternity of scholars is now dramatically opened. Students, working people, women concerned with change, nonwhites, lay persons and activists have begun to participate. While important assemblies of the dialogue were formerly held in Salzburg in 1965, Bavaria in 1966, Czechoslovakia in 1967 and in other Western and Eastern European nations, the trend of the future may be to hold such encounters in some of the Third World countries just mentioned (Yugoslavia, India, Tanzania, Mexico, Cuba, etc.). Here the participation will be by people who are functionally (versus structurally) related. The goal will be to illuminate and enrich each other's experience.

One other point needs to be made with respect to expanding participation. In the First and Second World communities, the movement of the dialogue from the university community to the urban community is barely under way. But lay persons and neo-Marxists will have to form the social base of the dialogue of the future here if it is to remain dynamic. Intellectually and ethically, they should become involved. Politically, it is almost a necessity that they do. Fanaticism and ignorance on both sides are simply not the conditions for the good life in the last third of the twentieth century; in fact, they are the preconditions for no life.

The new Marxist-Christian dialogue integrates the encounter. Now human existence, ecological conditions, technological change and ideology (utopian futuristic ideals) can begin to work together. The problems of human existence, an existence that is truly creative, are beginning to find an integrated expression in the world-wide encounter. Marxists and Christians from all three worlds face different problems associated with the human condition, and that reality requires a holistic perspective, not a fragmented one. Scarcity of necessities, pollution, automation and human purpose can and are being integrated in the new Marxist-Christian dialogue.

The Marxist-Christian dialogue itself is becoming slowly but surely an actor in the process of human development. What began as a *forum* for identification and clarification of issues is now an *actor* in the resolution of those problems. An analogy might be helpful to clarify this argument. The United Nations is frequently discussed in terms of its role as a forum of international politics, a place where the mighty and the miniscule states can talk together. It is less frequently viewed as an actor in international politics, but such is, of course, the case. This reality has been carefully developed and documented in a recent study of China and her U. N. policy.[21] The same holds true for the Marxist-Christian dialogue. Initially, it was exclusively a forum for discourse. Today, it is more—it is an actor that implements the conclusions reached at those discussions.

Finally, the new Marxist-Christian dialogue builds into the encounter a new moral dimension. The worldwide encounter today has assumed real responsibility. The enfeebling moral vacuum that characterized the old encounter has been filled by human activity. The result is a new vitality.

On the Human Individual. The existence of a new person—the Marxist Christian or Christian Marxist— has been mentioned. There simply are people who embrace both mentalities. If there are philosophical paradoxes involved, these people do not appear to be seriously hampered in their work as they go about the task of establishing the necessary human relationships that give meaning to these strange new conceptions. To the academic question "Can one be both a Marxist and a Christian?", we must now give the empirical answer "Yes."[22]

The position of the human being with respect to society is changing. New Marxists are shifting their focus from Marx's sociology to his anthropology to achieve the genuine balance necessary for an accurate interpretation. Radical Christians have rejected past practice and are redirecting their eyes from the Heavenly City to the Secular City.[23] The living, real, human, unique, active, actual individual is now the "point of departure." The social individual is the central measure of value. And man struggling toward a human future is the vision. The fiction of a proletariat without individuals and a church without people is rejected, as is the fantasy of an individual totally unrelated to other human beings.

That one can be both a Marxist and a Christian and that the human individual in history is important are the perceptions of dialogists that have a new personality. The dogmatism and authoritarianism that characterized the personality syndrome of Marxists and Christians during the twentieth century are giving way empirically to personality sets that are more open. The old closed cognitive systems of beliefs that generated the dogmatic and authoritarian personalities of Marxists and Christians are being replaced by open-ended sets of beliefs that allow for analysis, critique, correction and development of theology and theory.

The new Marxist-Christian dialogue alerts the people of all the world to their divided lives—alienated lives. Human beings who should find unity in their lives are instead fragmented into rigid, static roles that tolerate no breech of their parameters. The myths that coerce the human individual with respect to race, sex and labor are the central subjects of the new Marxist-Christian dialogue. This critique and the action to date to destroy these illusions is perhaps the most exciting new possibility of the encounter.

Lastly, the implication and possibility of a new conception of man, of the social and cooperative character of man, is being realized. The Marxist-Christian dialogue viewed from a worldwide perspective demonstrates the possibility that Marxists and Christians need not everlastingly conflict with one another, that, on the contrary, they can cooperate. These new relationships between people in different groups bear witness to the fact that the ideas that separate them are not as important as the humanity that unites them. Indeed, it is only when they forget the origin of their ideas in human history that they conduct themselves in an outrageous fashion. This cooperation between Marxists and Christians in all three worlds is empirically related to the Marxist-Christian dialogue. Given the reality of nuclear weapons, a history of hatred and ignorance, physical and cultural differences, and a technology that daily shrinks our little world to almost miniscule proportions, and given the fact that about one-half of the world's population subscribe to one or the other of the two belief systems discussed here, then certainly this new cooperation should be applauded.

On Society. Perhaps the most dramatic political implication of the new Marxist-Christian dialogue is in its "hidden agenda." The new Marxists and Christians involved in the encounter are questioning the concentration of authority in the party and the church. They are questioning the right of a privileged group to rule. They are demanding real equality as well as moral equality.

19

Granted that this commentary is only an indirect topic of concern in the First and Second World exchanges; it certainly is a direct topic in the Third World.

The major social implication of the new Marxist-Christian dialogue is that any new society we are to have on earth must be built by man and not wished or waited for. Christian utopian thought might heretofore be characterized as wishing for a new society, but wishing will not make it so. Communist utopian thought is just as idealistic, but it is best characterized as waiting. The economic base determines the ideological superstructure which, in turn, conditions man. All is inevitable and one need only wait for Communism to "break out." Both are distortions. Both are nonsense. The new society, if it is to be built, will be the result of cooperative human activity toward that goal. Christian longing and Communist patience will not work; only human activity can achieve the goal.

The organized party and church as social institutions are directly challenged by the new Marxist-Christian dialogue. The dialogists from all three worlds are clearly speaking and acting in a way that demands that these two formidable institutions begin to relate ends and means. To these new Marxists and Christians, the movement is the only reality. One is what one does, and no amount of rationalization can explain it away. Roger Garaudy, in his book *The Turning Point of Socialism*, has challenged the party.[24] Some of the leaders of the Roman Catholic hierarchy in Brazil have challenged the church.[25] Accountable decision-makers and bureaucracies, ideologically but not fanatically oriented, are necessary today in both groups. Part of the continuing challenge to these organized institutions emanates from the dialogue.

·The economic implications and future possibilities of the dialogue can be seen in the activities that took place in Chile recently. There Christians and Marxists employed Marx's socio-economic categories of analysis to understand the human and technological realities of Chile. The significance of human change and its relationship to the control of farms, transportation, tools, equipment and processes was demonstrated here. This kind of analysis does not augur well for those who exercise external control over another country's economic institutions. The Chilean experiment ended in a *coup d'etat*, but it sensitized the people of all Third World countries to the significance of controlling their own economic institutions. This new consciousness and understanding has had some important consequences already. Recently, "three Roman Catholic archbishops and eleven bishops have called for 'social ownership of the means of production' as the only way of ending widespread poverty in northwest Brazil."[26] Their thirty-page statement goes on to argue that Brazil's government "deludes most of Brazil's 100 million persons—95 percent of whom are Catholics—with propaganda about economic gains."[27]

The very positive role of Christian and Marxist believers in Yugoslavia, a socialist state, concerned with the establishment of human control over the critical economic aspect of their lives[28] is described in an essay by Paul Mojzes, the managing editor of *The Journal of Ecumenical Studies*.

On Marxist and Christian Thought. Perhaps the most

important consequence of the Marxist-Christian dialogue today is its tendency to de-mythologize theory and theology. Old myths, rituals, rigidities and falsehoods are beginning to give way to new developments in both systems of thought. Talk today is about models and revelancies *versus* invariable associations in important categories such as dialectics.[29] Static, mechanistic "ladders" to the Communist or Christian utopia, whether the Communist "5 step" or the Christian "7 step," are being rejected. Both groups of dialogists recognize that such explanations simply ignore time and change as aspects of historical reality.

Reaffirmation of the role of critique and the nature of the critical principle inherent in Marxism and Christianity is beginning to reinvigorate theory. As a result, ideological and theological fatigue is being replaced with new relevance. The new Marxists and Christians have abandoned the fanaticism of Stalinism and the Inquisition as well as the cynicism and indifference implied in these distortions and have opted for a humanized theory and theology. To them there are no more "sacred cows." There are no more categories about which one cannot speak. Incorrect thought should be corrected. Theory, such as the concept of alienation, that is only broadly outlined can now be developed. New categorical challenges can be openly confronted.

The restoration of the magnificent moral message inherent in Marxist and Christian thought brings back to each a humanized focus on the future goals as opposed to a concentration on immediate questions of control and authority. The praxis-oriented behavior of the young theologians and churchmen from the Second and Third Worlds when they protested against the Western-oriented focus and program of the World Council of Church's assembly on "Church and Society" in 1966 bears witness to this argument. The assembly of Marxists and Christians in Chile in 1972 does the same. Where one is going and how one gets there are both important questions in Marxism and Christianity. But the eschatological doctrine is crucial in the faith system of each body of thought, and there are few more eloquent statements of the nature and role of such radical hope than those included in the main essays of this book.

Finally, new parallels between Marxist and Christian thought in such categories as revolutionary change[30] as well as newly clarified differences in metaphysics and aesthetics are suggested in the worldwide encounter. The new dialogue demonstrates that Marxism is not an exercise in dogmatism and Christianity is not a doctrine of meditation. The new Marxist-Christian dialogue shows that both thought systems are in a process of change and that the rigid, puppet-like symbolism of the past will have no place in the future evolution of theory and theology.

The Relevance of This Book

The essays in this book are concrete illustrations of the new Marxist-Christian dialogue. The articles by Dr. Aptheker and Dr. Ogletree are fairly representative of the type presented in encounters in the First and Second Worlds. The nature and tone of the essay by Dr.

Bliss equally reflects the attitude and theme of most Third World participants—their impatience to "get going" on the job at hand.

Viewed as a whole, the book presents a truly dynamic expression of the nature and role of hope in human affairs and of the importance and utility of the eschatological doctrine. It clearly points out the major contribution of the Third World Marxist-Christian dialogue; i.e., it shows the First and Second World dialogists the limitations of an approach that is exclusively academic. It is nice to talk of liberation and hope, but we still have many hungry and homeless people. It is important to discuss love and the class struggle, but, again, we must still deal with people who lack clothing, fuel, medical service and education.

The past pointedly calls for human action that strives for perfection in history (Aptheker and Ogletree) and does something objectively to attain that goal (Bliss) *in a way* that corresponds to the finest ideal and activities of man throughout the centuries. The book points out the nature of the problem to date. The demand to ameliorate that condition now requires attention.

NOTES

1   Social scientists generally agree on the categories of classifying the nations of the world as follows: the First World is made up of the United States and its European friends; the Soviet Union and the Eastern European Communist nations compose the Second World; the Third World contains all the rest—the underdeveloped states of the world in Latin America, Asia, South Asia, Africa and the Near East. See Irving Louis Horowitz,

Three Worlds of Development. New York: Oxford University Press, 1966, pp. 3–46.

2   "Dialogue Between Catholics and Communists: Salzburg and Its Forerunners," *Herder Correspondence*, II (1965), 325–330; M. Bourdeaux, "Opening Dialogue," *Frontier*, Vol. IX (Autumn 1966), 203–205; Assembly in Prague, February 1962. Meeting between Christian theologians and Communist theorists to explore quietly the possibilities of encounter.

3   Kenneth A. Megill, *The New Democratic Theory.* New York: The Free Press, 1970, pp. 54–58; Roger Garaudy, *Marxism in The Twentieth Century.* New York: Charles Scribner's Sons, 1970, pp. 12–16; Thomas W. Ogletree, *Openings for Marxist-Christian Dialogue.* Nashville: Abingdon Press, 1969, pp. 33–44.

4   Douglas C. Stange, *The Nascent Marxist-Christian Dialogue: 1961–1967—A Bibliography.* American Institute for Marxist Studies, 1968.

5   Thomas W. Ogletree, *Openings for Marxist-Christian Dialogue*, p. 14.

6   Dieter Dux. *Ideology in Conflict.* New York: D. Van Nostrand Co., Inc., 1962, introduction.

7   M. Barth, "Developing Dialogue Between Marxist and Christian" (bibliography). *Journal of Ecumenical Studies*, Vol. IV (Summer 1967), pp. 385–405; M. Bourdeaux, "Dialogue with Marxists," *Frontier*, Vol. VIII (Autumn 1965), pp. 181–184; K. Develin, "Catholic-Communist Dialogue," *Problems of Communism*, Vol. XV (May 1966), pp. 31–38; Roger Garaudy, *From Anathema to Dialogue*, Chapters 2 and 3; A. T. Van Leevweir, "Christian-Marxist Dialogue," *Catholic World*, Vol. 208 (February 1969), pp. 219–21.

8   Rev. James Conway, *Today Show*, June 6, 1972.

9   Karl Marx, "Theses on Feuerbach," *Marx-Engels Selected Works*, II, pp. 403–405.

10   Holy Bible, Matthew 7:20, p. 674. London: Oxford University Press.

11   *Ibid.*, James 1:22 and 23, p. 851.

12   This particular concept, "good political work," was a

phrase employed by Professor Hillary Putnam, Department of Philosophy at Harvard University, in a speech at the University of Cincinnati on November 5, 1971.

13 Konrad Farner, "A Marxist View of Dialogue," *The Christian-Marxist Dialogue*, Paul Oestreicher, pp. 213–219; Zdenko Rotor, "A Marxist View of Christianity," *Journal of Ecumenical Studies*, Vol. 9 (Winter 1972), pp. 40–50.

14 Herbert Aptheker, *The Urgency of the Marxist-Christian Dialogue*. New York: Harper Colophon Books, 1970; Vjekoslav Bajsic, "The Significance and Problems of Dialogue Today," *Journal of Ecumenical Studies*, Vol. 9 (Winter 1972), p. 29.

15 Roger Garaudy, *From Anathema to Dialogue*. New York: Vintage Books, 1968, pp. 79–82.

16 J. Moltmann, "The Rendition of Freedom," *Openings for Marxist-Christian Dialogue*, Thomas Ogletree, pp. 51–53. Nashville: Abingdon, 1969.

17 Rosemary Ruether, *The Radical Kingdom*. New York: Harper and Row, 1970, Chap. 1.

18 Adam Schaff, *Marxism and the Human Individual*. New York: The McGraw-Hill Book Co., 1970. See especially Chap. 1.

19 Leszek Kolakowski, "What Socialism is Not," *The Christian-Marxist Dialogue*, Oestreicher, pp. 165–169.

20 S. A. Garcia, C. Calle (ed.), *Camilo Torres: Priest and Revolutionary*. London: Sheed and Ward, 1968.

21 Byron S. J. Weng, *Peking's U. N. Policy: Continuity and Change*. New York: Praeger Publishers, 1972, especially Part I.

22 Conway, *Today Show*, June 6, 1972.

23 Harvey Cox, *The Secular City*. New York: The Macmillan Co., 1965.

24 Roger Garaudy, *The Turning Point of Socialism*. London: Fontana/Collins, 1969.

25 *International Herald Tribune*, May 21, 1973, p. 2.

26 *Ibid.*

27 *Ibid.*

28   Paul Mojzes, "Christian–Marxist Encounter in the Con-
     text of a Socialist Society," *Journal of Ecumenical
     Studies*, Vol. 9 (Winter 1972), pp. 1–28.

29   Roger Garaudy, *From Anathema to Dialogue*, Chap. III.

30   Rosemary Ruether, *The Radical Kingdom*.

SUGGESTIONS FOR FURTHER READING

Roger Garaudy, *The Turning-Point of Socialism.* London:
  Fontana/Collins, 1969.

Karl Marx and Friedrich Engels, *On Religion.* New York:
  Schocken Books, 1964.

Adam Schaff, *Marxism and the Human Individual.* New
  York: McGraw-Hill Book Company, 1970.

Charles West, *Communism and the Theologians.* New York:
  The Macmillan Company, 1958.

WHAT MAY MAN REALLY HOPE FOR?

HERBERT APTHEKER

Before addressing myself to the major topic, I shall make a few comments on the process and significance of the dialogue between Marxists and Christians. The Marxist and Christian worldviews are adhered to by about half of mankind. Any dialogue among adherents of world views that command such a following is consequential. But when, in addition, the dialogue concerns itself, as it must, with interests and issues central to both, it simultaneously concerns itself with issues that are central to that half of the world population which may be conjectured as holding to neither the Marxist nor the Christian view. Finally, since the Marxist and Christian outlooks continue to have substantial differences and since these differences continue to evoke fierce mutual antagonism, it is surely cause for high hope that today in many parts of the world Marxists and Christians have deliberately sought civilized discourse with each other. Moreover, they have sought this dialogue, not to score points or win over an opponent, but to comprehend each other, learn from each other, and undertake to discover likenesses as well as differences, the better to help create a less destructive human order.

Something of the history of this dialogue—and it already has had a considerable history—was told by Mr. Ogletree himself in his introduction to an admirable and challenging volume which he edited and which was published in 1969.[1] How significant the dialogue has become may be indicated by the fact that the *Reader's Digest*, chief organ of the *status quo*, recently devoted a two-part article to explaining to the magazine's 19 million readers how awful and devious "were such talk fests between clergy and Communists."[2]

On an entirely different level, Boston College, a Jesuit institution, now offers graduate degrees in Marxist Studies and held a summer session in 1972 entitled "Institute on Marxist Thought," which was conducted by six visiting scholars and four of the college's faculty members. I must confess that, though I am optimistic, I did not think when establishing the American Institute for Marxist Studies in New York City in 1964, in order to move, as our prospectus then said, from "diatribe to dialogue," that in less than ten years a Roman Catholic college in the United States would be offering graduate degrees in Marxist Studies and would be conducting an institute on Marxist thought of a most *catholic* character.

This development affords an exhilarating note upon which to enter into a consideration of our subject, "What May Man Really Hope For?" I would like to say a few words about the title. I do not use the word *man* as the founders of this Republic did when they affirmed in the Declaration of Independence that all *men* are created equal. They meant *men* and not *women*, as Abigail Adams did not fail to point out to her husband John. I use the word *man* to mean *people*, to mean *human beings.* Important in the title also are the words *really hope for.* Presumably this phrase means that the discussion should be what is called "realistic" and not "utopian." I will reserve for later some thoughts I have on "utopianism" and its connection with what is called "realistic." At this point, however, I assume that the word *really* suggests that we should strive in this dialogue for that great American virtue, practicality. I believe, too, that the word is meant to impart a certain secular quality to our dialogue, so that we are not to get into questions of salvation, eternity, heaven and hell, but are to concern ourselves with realistic possibilities for humanity on earth and in the foreseeable future. Assuming that my defining efforts are correct, I will now turn to the matter at hand.

In religion as a whole, I believe, certainly not least in Christianity, a tension exists between prophet and priest, between challenging the *status quo* and bulwarking it. The Italian scholar, Vittorio Lanternari, in his fine study of what he calls modern messianic cults, sees their appearance as reflections of the drive for liberation from colonialism. In this sense, Mr. Lanternari writes, "they provide one of the most startling demonstrations of the close ties between religious life and secular, political and cultural life." "The cults," he says, "represent so many cries for freedom, and insofar as they do, constitute an indictment of Western civilization."[3] He adds that these cults are similar in origin to all the great religions—Buddhism, Taoism, Judaism, Islam and Christianity. "Each," he reminds us, "began as a prophetic movement of renewal," stimulated by given cultural and social conditions in a time of crisis. "The striving for religious renewal and liberation," he writes, "arises from the rebellion of the masses against existing official cults imposed by ruling castes."[4]

Engels himself called attention several times to what he called "the notable points of resemblance between early Christianity and the working-class movements of modern history." Engels noted that "the essential feature" of Christianity at its beginning was its partisanship towards the poor, the despised, the enslaved, and the oppressed, a partisanship that, Engels wrote, "reverses the world order."[5]

Early Christianity, as befits its revolutionary character and composition, denounced the ruling gods and so was called atheist, excoriated the secular powers and so was called seditious, upbraided the rich and so was called deluded, pointed to private property and the accumulation of profit and its twin, covetousness, as the chief source of evil and so was called a dangerous madness to be extirpated from the earth. Near Carthage in the year 295, Maximilian was brought before the authorities to be measured and conscripted for army service. But, he said, "I cannot serve, I cannot do wrong, I am a Christian." The authorities pleaded with him and urged his father to advise him, but his father replied that Maximilian was old enough to know his own duty. The proconsul pleaded again, pointing out that others who called themselves Christians served in the army. When Maximilian still refused, the official persisted, "But those who serve, what wrong do they do?" For Maximilian, however, such matters were beyond argument, and when he continued to refuse, he was sentenced "to die by the sword." The record stated that he was "21 years old, 3 months and 18 days." On his way to execution, Maximilian urged that the suit prepared for his army service be given with his compliments to his executioner. A woman, known to history only as Polmya, accompanied him to his execution and was permitted to claim his body. She herself died twelve days later. The father held firm and gloried in the strength of his son.[6]

True to the example of Maximilian, nine Christian men and women, priests and laymen, announced in May, 1968, at Catonsville, Maryland, that they were burning the draft records of that community with napalm. They asserted, "We take the Christian gospel seriously. We, therefore, are indicting all religions of the United States for being racist, guilty of complicity in war and hostile to the poor." They were, they said, "appalled by the ruse of the American ruling class invoking pleas for law and order to mask and perpetuate injustice." They closed, "We have pleaded, spoken, marched, and nursed the victims of their injustice. Now this injustice we think must be faced, and this we intend to do with whatever strength of mind, body and grace God will give us. May God have mercy upon our nation."[7]

Count Metternich and John Brown both affirmed piety. Jefferson Davis and Nat Turner both thought of themselves as Christians. As the societal crises deepen, the tension between the prophetic and the priestly characterizes the religious crisis of our era. As the Catonsville example indicates, cleavage in the United States centers on questions of foreign policy and domestic racism. In March, 1971, a Roman Catholic Church assembly in Italy's nothernmost province, Alto Adige,

32

adopted a statement affirming that Marxism was more pleasing to God than capitalism. Marxist concepts, according to this assembly, appear more attuned to God's plan than capitalist society. One may well believe the *New York Times* correspondent, Paul Hoffman, who reported from Rome that "the Vatican theologians were examining this pro-Marxist doctrine with great and somewhat puzzled care and that it had attracted nationwide attention." (*New York Times*, March 10, 1971)

In May, 1972, an inter-American assembly entitled "Christians for Socialism" attracted 400 cleric and lay participants from every Latin American country except Brazil and Bolivia, where, to quote the *New York Times*, May 4, "left-wing priests have been under severe police control." This assembly endorsed what it called "a strategic alliance with Marxists for the purpose of achieving socialism throughout Latin America." The resolution of this assembly said, "Socialism appears to be the only acceptable alternative for bringing an end to the exploitation of class society," and it added, "to arrive at socialism requires more than a critical theory of capitalism. It also requires revolutionary action by the working class and a strategy that leads to the takeover of power." The major organizer of this assembly in Chile was a Jesuit priest, Father Gonzalo Oroyo. This assembly conveys some idea of the urgency of Marxist-Christian dialogue.

If Latin America should strike anyone in the United States as being remote, I suggest that this feeling may be due to a provincialism whose existence in the United States has always been costly, but is now verging on the disastrous. The crisis at home has reached a stage where

Senator Fulbright, Chairman of the Foreign Relations Committee, can affirm that our society "is a sick one," where the dean of United States journalists and publicists, Walter Lippmann, can assert that, in his half century as an analyst and observer, "the present condition of the United States is the worst I have ever seen," and where Senator Adlai Stevenson II, of Illinois, can declare that "our foreign policy is largely bankrupt." This grave situation suggests the propriety, not to say necessity, of a radical critique of dominant U. S. policy and priorities, perhaps even the relevancy of the Marxist insight to the present-day United States.

One often hears that both Marxism and Christianity should be dismissed because they represent dreams that sound good but have little in common with the hard and practical requirements of this tough world. I hold that "utopianism" serves a very practical function in the world. By "utopianism" I mean striving for perfection or for what is conceived of as perfection. Indeed, to live on tiptoes, I suggest, is the best way to live. In any case, as Aristotle held, to strive for perfect happiness does not mean that such perfection is attainable; rather it means that it is a valid goal in life and that the striving for it is a worthwhile manner in which to conduct one's life. Similarly, the effort to make a heaven on earth, to make the earth perfect here, even as it is in heaven, may not be achieveable, but the striving for it is wonderful, and the effort to achieve it will surely bring us nearer to justice than if we do not strive at all. The Jewish prophets insisted, "Let justice be done, though the very heavens fall." Impractical on its face, no doubt, but marvelously invigorating in the struggle against injustice and a splendid ideal for the leading of a truly worthwhile life, *i.e.*, one that is, in this sense, truly practical.

Marxists urge the achieving of a classless society, devoid of exploitation, devoid of authority over people, and marked by rational control over institutions. "Where is there such a society?" one is often asked in derision. But then Marxism is but a century old, and efforts in creating socialist societies are only half a century old. Perhaps in this time, it is not unfair to suggest that Marxists have come at least as near to achieving their goals as have Christians in the 2,000 years they have so far had at their disposal.[8]

Marxists and Christians are agreed not only on a certain utopian bent; they are agreed, also, on certain basic ethical assumptions, and this agreement is surely relevant to the question before us: "What May Man Really Hope For?" Several of these assumptions have been articulated recently by Professor John Somerville of California Western University.[9]

1. Continued life is better than death, except with one's own considered wish and consent.
2. Pleasure is better than pain, except where the pain brings greater pleasure.
3. Health is better than sickness.
4. Employment at the level of qualifications is better than involuntary unemployment.
5. Material sufficiency or abundance is better than poverty or deprivation.
6. Knowledge is better than ignorance.
7. The development of one's creative capacities, so long as this is not inherently injurious to others, is better than their stultification.

Other propositions could be added on which there is general agreement. For example, treating all people with respect, regardless of their race or sex, is preferable to racist or male chauvinist behavior.

If virtual unanimity exists on these ethical standards, then significant ground emerges for a positive response to the question posed for our discussion. Perhaps this optimism will become persuasive if I can spell out a national program that implements the goals implied in these propositions. Such a program would clearly benefit most Americans, is needed, and would bring our society to the threshold of socialism. At any rate, though I am not now running for public office, I make bold to offer this detailed and specific program and to suggest that it is what man, in the United States in the 1970's, may really hope for.

Though not exhaustive, I submit that the following program is basic, that it gets to the heart of people's real problems:

1. Better housing.
2. More nurseries and kindergartens at no or minimum cost.
3. More parks.
4. Lower rents and utility rates.
5. Lower taxes for the poor.
6. Massive appropriations for social well-being.
7. An adequate guaranteed yearly income.
8. Free medical care for all.
9. A decisive assault upon the scandal of hunger and poverty to be significantly planned and controlled by those who suffer from both.
10. The purification of the police and the courts, with the people over both, and not both over the people.

11. An end to unemployment.
12. A major redesign of the public welfare system, with the recipients in charge of the transformation.
13. An educational system cleansed of racism, elitism, chauvinism, and snobbishness, with all schools free to all people and with the goal of quality education.
14. An end to all discrimination against women.
15. Measures to encourage youth in their righteous demands for creativity and relevance.
16. Democratization of the political and party structures at all levels.
17. Strict enforcement of present anti-racist laws, especially the Fourteenth and Fifteenth Amendments to the Constitution and severe penalties for all manifestations of racism.
18. Nationalization of all armaments production.
19. High taxes for the rich and no tax loopholes.
20. A militant drive to organize the unorganized workers.
21. Repeal of all state and federal anti-labor, anti-union and so-called anti-subversive boards and laws.
22. Freedom for all political prisoners, particularly those victimized by racial injustice and those heroic people in or out of uniform who have been jailed or exiled for refusing to fight in the unspeakably vile war conducted by the government of the United States in Indochina.
23. Complete redirection of U.S. foreign policy from one that seeks to destroy the national liberation struggles of colonial peoples and to contain and roll back socialism to a policy which supports anti-imperialist struggles throughout the world.
24. End to U.S. militarism, in particular to the draft, the dismantling of overseas bases, an end to all atomic and nuclear weapons testing, the return of all U.S. soldiers from abroad, and the immediate and full withdrawal of U.S. forces from Indochina.

25. A United States foreign policy which boycotts the Republic of South Africa and inaugurates trade with the Republic of Cuba.

A system condemns itself, in my opinion, when Senator Eastland receives a subsidy of $13,000 a month from the federal government for not growing cotton on his plantations while, in the same state of Mississippi, an impoverished child receives from that state $9 a month. A system condemns itself when the infant mortality rate in the richest neighborhood of Detroit is 12.1 per 1,000 while in the city's poorest section it is 69.1 per 1,000. This last statistic is a measure of institutionalized violence—in this case, a violence concentrated upon the killing of infants. Yet those who maintain and profit from such a system have the gall to lecture others about law and order and the use of violence.

In its dedication to the struggle against social evils still afflicting the majority of the human race, Marxism knows and emphasizes that its goals are fundamentally the same as those held by the partisans of the Enlightenment and upholders of all the great religions. Were we Marxists alone in this struggle, we would persevere in it, but we would fail. We are not alone, however. All who stand together opposed to systematized exploitation and the systematic extermination known as war will, to the degree that they maintain such unity, overcome the forces of evil and fulfill the promise of mankind. This is what, in my opinion, man may really hope for now. It is certainly that for which all human beings should strive.

NOTES

1 *Openings for Marxist-Christian Dialogue.* Nashville: Abingdon Press, 1969.

2 Several important American citizens were blatantly misrepresented in this article. One of them, Professor Martin Marty, made comments on the article in the "Pen-ultimate" column of *The Christian Century* (October 27, 1971).

3 *The Religions of the Oppressed,* Lisa Sergio, trans. New York: Alfred Knopf, 1965. Published first in Rome in 1960.

4 *Ibid.*

5 These quotations are from "Bauer and Early Christianity" (1882) and "On the History of Early Christianity" (1885); see my *The Urgency of Marxist-Christian Dialogue.* New York: Harper and Row, 1970, pp. 2, 3.

6 Jacque Zeller, *Christian Beginnings.* New York: Hawthorne Books, 1960, pp. 177–80.

7 Philip Berrigan, S. J., *A Punishment for Peace.* New York: Macmillan, 1969, pp. 171–74.

8 For an insightful discussion on the practical functions of utopianism, see: George H. Hampsch, "Dignity, Social Power and Classless Society," *The Philosophy Forum,* Vol. 10 (December 1971), pp. 277–291.

9 "Human Dignity, Human Rights and War," *Philosophy Forum,* Vol. 9, No. 4 (1971), p. 13.

SUGGESTIONS FOR FURTHER READING

Herbert Aptheker, *Marxism and Christianity.* New York: Humanities Press, 1968.

————, *The Urgency of the Marxist-Christian Dialogue.* New York: Harper and Row, 1970.

Roger Garaudy, *From Anathema to Dialogue.* New York: Vintage Books, 1968.

Leszek Kolakowski, *Toward a Marxist Humanism.* Grove Press, Inc., 1968.

WHAT MAY MAN REALLY HOPE FOR?

THOMAS W. OGLETREE

Before turning to the substantive question, I shall offer some reflections on the difference between debate and dialogue. People debate when they think they already have the answers. There is an issue. I know what my side is, and I am convinced it is right. My job is to convince my opponent I am right, or if I cannot convince him, I seek to defeat him with my arguments so that other people will see that my view is better than his. Dialogue is very different. You engage in dialogue when you encounter another person or another perspective with the expectation of mutual benefit, of mutual growth in understanding. You engage in dialogue when you do not think you have all the answers, when you sense some of the perplexities of life, when you are puzzled about important issues, when, for example, you are seeking the best way to deal with the suffering and agony of human beings. We are attempting to bring together our insights and resources out of a variety of traditions and experiences in order to find our way through the critical problems we face in our contemporary world. That is what we are about in this exchange.

When I encounter Marxism, I do not proceed with the assumption that Christianity and Marxism are necessarily opposed, that you must give allegiance to one or the other. Many Christians consider themselves Marxists. They do not see Christianity and Marxism as two perspectives on life at all; they rather see them as two dimensions of a common perspective—Marxism contributing certain features that Christianity needs and Christianity contributing things that are not adequately considered or developed in Marxism. The concern of such people is to hold both together. Broadly speaking, I would have to characterize myself in this way. My own study of Marxism profoundly influences my life as I try to think through the way I situate myself in the world in which I live. I cannot call myself a Marxist. I think there is something a little bit odd about such a designation. I am not even sure Marx would consider himself a Marxist, if that means some final allegiance to a given view of things. However, as a style of approaching a troubled world and of trying to work one's way through that world as responsibly and humanly as possible, Marxism is a perspective which must indeed be taken seriously. I think it is a tragedy that Marx's questions and general approaches to human suffering and to social difficulties have not been appreciated more fully within the United States. Perhaps the dominance of capitalism and our need to justify and legitimate our form of social order as the superior way of life have prevented a more positive appraisal of Marxism.

Now for the central question, "What can we really hope for?" It seems to me that we are on common ground when we recognize, as the ancient proverb put it, "where there is no hope, the people perish." Keeping hope alive among people who see oppression and hurt and destruction everywhere has become exceedingly difficult. The danger of losing hope is one of the things that particularly concerns me at the present time. Many people are giving up on the possibility of being able to do anything at all about our world's problems. They seek to escape an oppressive social situation by moving wholly into the private sector, perhaps withdrawing into communal life where they can be a little bit more human. They feel there is nothing more they can do about the massive problems that confront our society or the larger world community. Sustaining hope has become a desperately urgent problem. That is the focus of our discussion.

When we look at the content of hope as it comes out of the Christian tradition, we can lift up some very basic terms which have some positive meaning for most of us, terms such as liberation, or reconciliation, or peace, or wholeness of life. The Christian faith, along with many of the great religions of the world, holds out for mankind hope for fullness of life, for reconciliation, for liberation from the things that enslave and bind us, for a power that can offer completeness to us in our existence.

When I look at the hope of the Christian tradition, I have to say that it does not concern a simple "this-worldly" future which I can project; yet for Christians it is nonetheless real. The hope is that beyond our historical experience in its brokenness there is a possibility of participating in the fullness of God where all the evils of this world have been taken up and overcome. It concerns the unification of all things in the divine life, where God is all in all. This motif is a very crucial feature of Christian hope. If we say we are not going to talk about man's "ultimate" hope, we may be putting aside one of the decisive features of the Christian understanding. To make the point negatively, the Christian hope reminds us that man cannot find fulfillment in his total being by the creation of *any conceivable* society. Any society we are able to bring into being is going to have its own distortions, its own brokenness, its own ambiguity, its own pain, its own incompleteness. One of our needs is to find a ground of hope that can enable us to endure humanly in the face of the everpresent ambiguities and pains of existence which we can never finally overcome.

At the same time, if the Christian hope is to be understood adequately, it can in no sense be restricted to the ultimate participation of all creation in the divine life. It must also continually be understood as a present reality qualifying our life in this world, sustaining us in our secular existence as we face everyday problems and struggle to overcome very specific and concrete wrongs by projecting and working to realize alternative historical futures. Both of these dimensions and levels of hope are essential parts of the Christian hope when it is understood in its fullness: the ultimate religious hope and the concrete social hope. I regard Marxism as important because it can help me understand what is at stake in struggling for the concrete, historical expressions of human hope. The meaning of this struggle has become more clear to me from studying Marx. Let me underscore the contrast I have in mind. Christian hope involves (1) an ultimate religious hope of participation in the divine life, but it also involves (2) ever-new forms of concrete historical expression of that ultimate hope.

If I am going to take seriously the hope of liberation promised to me in faith, then I have got to be engaged in concrete liberation struggles in this world. As a matter of fact, I do not think I can know what the liberation of men in the Kingdom of God means if I have not been involved in struggling with very specific chains that enslave people in my own society—the chains of racism, the chains of poverty, the chains of male privilege, the chains of imperialism, the chains of a bureaucratic society that bind us to dehumanizing tasks. Unless I am participating in these struggles, I cannot understand the content of the ultimate promise of liberation. I must have both dimensions of hope in their interaction in order to know the meaning of Christian hope.

Marxism can give social reality and substance to the concrete, historical expressions of religious hope. Marx exposed illusory hopes. This activity constituted his negative task. He particularly assailed the understandings of religious hope that were simply and purely "other worldly." He showed how a hope that is simply and purely "other worldly" functions to leave the present order of life *as is*. Such a hope ceases to be critical of the present order. It accepts the injustice and the bondage of that order. It no longer troubles itself with "worldly" matters. Naturally, those who benefit from the present order of things are going to have a lot at stake in selling people on a purely "other worldly" understanding of Christian hope. Marx exposed this fact— that an ultimate religious hope without a concrete social hope is empty and, finally, phony.

I think Marx equally wanted to expose the kind of utopianism which consists of dreaming about an ideal

44

world we would like to have, laying out a magnificent program to bring it into being, and then trying to persuade everyone to work for it. Marx has clearly shown that this procedure is also a false way to go. We have little chance of doing anything concrete to improve the situation of man by following this approach. Christian people and humanist people have been tempted to deal with hope in a utopian fashion. That, too, is illusory dreaming. We cannot convince people to support our magnificent programs simply because they share the great ideals which these programs are supposed to implement—peace, liberation for all people, justice, human dignity.

It is not enough simply to talk about beautiful ideals. Marx argued that we must be hardheaded analysts of the real situation that human beings find themselves in if we want to improve the human condition. We have got to see the social sources of human oppression. We have got to see why and how people are being torn apart by our society. Indeed, it is not enough simply to discover the social causes of human suffering and on that basis propose a cure. We have got to see the forces at work in a situation that give us some reason for believing that privileged power can be broken. It is not enough to analyze the causes of a bad situation and then design a program to correct it, for there are always some people, usually powerful and influential people, who benefit from the way things are. Such persons are going to oppose any program or subvert any program that seriously starts getting at those root causes. If we are interested in improving the conditions of human life, we have got to identify and ally ourselves with

45

social forces capable of breaking open an unjust and oppressive situation so that some new possibilities can be brought into being.

Marx teaches us to look at the points of strain, the points of conflict, the points of contradiction in society, because there are the points where the fragility and weakness of a seemingly powerful social order shows itself. When we address the weaknesses in the present order, we have the possibility of aligning ourselves with movements which can bring into being a new kind of reality. The new reality comes not so much from projecting ideal programs, but more from identifying social forces at work in a situation that have the promise of enabling us to transcend what is unjust about the present order.

Marx rightly saw that the people most victimized by an existing state of affairs usually understand most profoundly—at a human level—what their problems are. I do not mean that such persons have the best understanding of these problems in terms of sophisticated intellectual analysis. Their understanding is deepest in terms of the "gut-level" experience. The oppressed, moreover, are the ones who have the most energy to stay in the battle for a new state of affairs. It is not surprising that new creation in human social existence repeatedly comes from the oppressed, from the proletariat, whoever they are. I believe a certain moral precedence should be given to people who are battling out of a situation of oppression. That is why we rightly identify black Americans and other racial and cultural minorities as the ones who offer us the best promise of regaining our soul as a people, of discovering anew the promise of our land. That is also why students have been the toughest battlers to end the Vietnam war; they are the ones who have had the most at stake personally in seeing that this war came to an end.

Marx has taught me that it is not enough simply to *talk* about liberation or peace or reconciliation. I must also identify the real forces working for changes in my situation and become a part of those forces. Otherwise, I am not engaged in living out the hope for liberation and wholeness and peace for all mankind which finds expression in the ultimate religious hope. Marx gave us a beautiful model for understanding this kind of process in his analysis of nineteenth-century capitalism and in his very penetrating studies of the class struggles in France in the nineteenth century. I think these are magnificent works. I do not believe we can simply repeat Marx's specific judgments, because the situations he was describing do not exist anymore, at least not in the same form. Rather, we must learn ourselves to be critical thinkers in relation to our own situation. We must find ways of sustaining and supporting and being a part of critical struggles within our society. Without this kind of concrete historical form, the ultimate religious hope of which I spoke becomes empty; it becomes a deceit, it becomes something which people concerned about the well-being of their fellows must condemn. People who have the most at stake in maintaining the present order are the ones most tempted to identify the Christian hope solely with its ultimate expression. People involved with the prophetic task are the ones who understand the equal urgency of concrete historical expressions of the ultimate hope.

47

Nevertheless, it is also not enough, in my judgment, to talk about man's hopes simply in terms of concrete, historical possibilities for overcoming specific, social injustices. At this point, I find myself in basic agreement with the list of social changes that Dr. Aptheker would like to bring to fruition. If I am uneasy about the list, it is chiefly because of its utopian sound, not because of its content. It does not sound like a Marxist way of dealing with the future. It talks about programs without examining the way people's vital interests are related to those programs. There are many people who benefit by the very injustices these programs are aimed at overcoming. They will naturally use their resources to make sure that such program goals are not realized. Still, for my part, I want to affirm such programs. I would like to see them come about, and I want myself to be a part of efforts that give us some chance of moving in that direction. But I do not believe it is enough for me as a human being to live simply by such hopes. I do not think such hopes can finally be sufficient for me. *Even if every item in that program were to be realized, I do not believe we would necessarily know the wholeness of life for which we yearn.* Even in that frame of reference, we would find new expressions of injustice, new forms of exploitation, new patterns of privilege. We would find that some of the things which looked innocent and good on the surface brought in new problems we never dreamed of. We do not have enough imagination or knowledge to see all the implications of our programs. In other words, no matter how successful we may be in realizing the noblest programs, we will still find that there is a great deal of ambiguity, a great deal of injustice, and a great deal of suffering which leaves us incomplete. There is a hunger for wholeness of life which always goes beyond any concrete historical realization of the human quest for fulfillment. That "going beyond" is itself a genuine part of human hope. This point is the main one I want to make here. It, too, must be taken seriously. It indicates the human basis of the ultimate religious hope about which I have spoken.

This ultimate religious hope can have some very important consequences for the way we engage in concrete, historical struggles. It can sustain us and undergird us amid all of the insecurity, fraility and vulnerability which we experience as we participate in those struggles. If we know that there is a hope of fullness of life for us at the deepest levels of our being, whether we realize our programs or not, we have a new kind of freedom to be in those struggles, a freedom which enables us to invest our lives in spite of our frailty and vulnerability. The ultimate religious hope can also remind us of the relativity of all our human projections. The solutions we propose for particular problems are always relative to those problems and always relative to given situations. But history keeps moving on and presenting us with new sets of problems. I may at times get so zealously committed to some of these concrete, historical programs that I absolutize them, talk about them as though they were going to solve everybody's problem, now and forever. Then I deceive myself. Moreover, if I do absolutize my programs, I am more apt to be ruthless and destructive in my quest to bring them about. The ultimate religious hope can be a continual lure to maintain a critical role in relationship to society.

It is a reminder that I can never rest content with any concrete realization; I must always be addressing new expressions of human bondage, conflict and suffering, and searching for appropriate ways to deal with those problems.

Finally, this ultimate religious hope is something that can sustain us in the face of crushing defeat, and defeat does come upon us again and again. I remember talking with a student some years ago who said, "Why are you still interested in politics? I tried politics and it didn't do any good." What he meant was that he worked in McCarthy's campaign for president, but McCarthy did not even get nominated, let alone elected. When we get defeated in a concrete struggle, our spirits are often broken, especially if we have worked very hard and made costly sacrifices. Our continued temptation is to yield to that brokenness in despair. The power of an ultimate religious hope can sustain us even in the midst of despair. Frankly, I think that a great deal of the power of the black liberation movement in this country comes from such a hope. Black Americans have probably sustained more crushing defeat and more exploitation in this country than any other group of people, except perhaps the American Indians. Yet they have displayed a sturdy, triumphant kind of hope in the face of those defeats which has enabled them to persist as one of the most formidable forces for social change within our own society. The hope of which I speak enables me to say, "Life is worthwhile; it has significance. Even this broken, frail, twisted world is worth living in, and I want to be a part of it in spite of the defeats. I want to be a part of it even in the midst of the defeats, because there is something good about living." This is precisely the kind of hope that can over the long haul make us sturdier warriors in the struggle for social justice in spite of the vulnerability and impotence we experience in that struggle.

My contention is that we need both levels of hope in order to be realistic—the ultimate religious hope and the concrete historical hope. The Marxists have provided us with a model for giving social reality and substance to the concrete historical expressions of hope. But this level of hope cannot in my judgment legitimately abolish the human significance of a more ultimate level of hope.

SUGGESTIONS FOR FURTHER READING

Jürgen Moltmann, *Religion, Revelation and the Future,* trans. by M. Douglas Meeks. New York: Charles Scribner's Sons, 1969.

Paul Oestreicher, *The Christian-Marxist Dialogue.* London: The Macmillan Company, 1969.

Thomas W. Ogletree, *Openings for Marxist-Christian Dialogue.* Nashville: Abingdon Press, 1969.

RESPONSE

HERBERT APTHEKER

I know that the problem of ultimate hope (salvation) exists, but I do not deal with it as a live option. Of course, we do find in the history of Christianity the two-fold Christian concept of hope that Mr. Ogletree put forth. However, the Marxist rejects this view. Marxism is atheistic.

Because of this rejection, quite a few people, especially in the United States, think that Marxists are moral idiots. On the other hand, there are some sectarian so-called Marxists who think that anybody who is not a Marxist is just a plain idiot. But attitudes of this kind preclude all possibility of dialogue.

"Why is Marxism atheistic?" There are several reasons. One is what we like to think of as a scientific view, an insistence upon empirical proof and empirical reality. From the philosophical view, Marxism is materialist. Dialectical materialism rejects all forms of philosophical idealism, and religion, no matter how defined, is idealistic in the technical, philosophical sense. According to the materialist view of the problem of causation, consciousness does not precede reality; materiality induces ideas, not the other way around. This position is fundamental to Marxism and absolutely basic to its program of determining what is wrong in society and how to correct it. Racism, for instance, is a system of ideas. It is not self-made; no child is born a racist. Racism is a system of ideas induced socially—induced historically. Therefore, racism is subject to remedy, but not to the Myrdalian-Elkins-Freudian remedy of putting everybody on a couch. Who is going to be the psychiatrist in a racist society? Besides, there is not enough time nor are there enough couches to do the job. Meanwhile, black people are crucified while everyone is on the couch.

It is more important to seek to understand the historic and socioeconomic sources of the problem in order to effect change. We must wipe out the swamp in which malaria-carrying mosquitos breed. That prescription defines a fundamental philosophical position. In this sense, then, Marxism is atheistic.

A second reason for rejecting the concept of ultimate hope is that this concept, in our opinion, denigrates man. Man creates God, not vice versa. How magnificent is man that he can have a conception of God—but it *is* man's conception. Moreover, we do not need anything outside ourselves. On the contrary, we insist that affirming such a need weakens us, debases us, distorts us.

Therefore, we reject concepts of salvation. This rejection has sometimes been expressed stupidly, vulgarly, mechanically, insultingly and without comprehension, partially because we have not had these kinds of dialogues. Nevertheless, the argument against such concepts is necessary.

Professor Ogletree contends that one must have a concept of hope (salvation) in order to deal constructively with his experience of perpetual brokenness. But we are not told why. I suppose this assertion is made because it has always been made by theologians. In that case, the assertion does not rest on a very scientific argument, but then I suppose we are not discussing science. But even suppose that perpetual brokenness is to be our lot. The point is that we must learn to endure in the face of pain. How do I endure in the face of pain? Or do you think I don't endure, or do you think I don't suffer pain? How did Marx endure with three children who were in constant poverty and hunger? How did Lenin endure? How did Fuchik endure when the Gestapo cut off his head? How do a thousand comrades endure? How does Angela endure? Does this alleged need for some ultimate hope argue against Nat Turner and the way he endured? He endured because he spat in the faces of his jailers, and he said, "Was Christ crucified?" when they asked him if he was guilty. "No, I'm not guilty. Was Christ crucified?" Angela does not say, "Was Christ crucified?" Angela says, "I am not guilty." She is not broken. We are able to endure pain. Do not think that we cannot or have not had it or do not understand it. We think we may better endure pain. The glory of the struggle is in the struggle.

The glory of the struggle, that's the thing—comradeship! The sense of strength that some individuals find in religion I experience in struggle and in combat. You can find the glory of this struggle and this comradeship in organizing sharecroppers in Georgia when you are attacked by the KKK and you know that one comrade will die for another. If you haven't had such a feeling, you haven't lived. Now, I am sure you may have that feeling in religion, but I assure you that I have also had it and understand it, and it nerves my actions. It is because of

54

this joy in struggle and comradeship that the Vietnamese have been able to resist napalm. Johnson said they are a bunch of naked brown dwarfs armed with knives and that we must take the knives from them. Well, they may be short-statured, and they are certainly brown, but we have had a hell of a time taking the knives away from them, haven't we? And they are nerved by Marxism. They are my comrades. I fight with them. I went there in 1965. So it is the struggle itself.

Marxism holds forth no final solution. Hence, the program which I projected here was a program that man may really struggle to achieve now in the 1970's, and in that struggle itself you can find wholeness.

Tom Ogletree is absolutely correct, of course, in pointing to the possibility of reification and fanaticism, but fanaticism is not Marxism. Marxism, like any conception, is subject to stultification, ossification, and fanaticism, but not authentic Marxism. Marxism insists on criticism and self-criticism. It is also an organizational principle. Marxism is science. There is no greater compliment to a scientist than the discovery of error. That's what science is about. Science advances through the discovery of error, doesn't it? Isn't that how sciences advance? Of course, Marxism is a conception, a dialectical materialist conception, which must be applied critically, self-critically, to a particular area, a particular time. Anyone who thought socialism would be the same in Cuba as it is in Bulgaria is a fool or a C. I. A. agent.

Professor Ogletree was very generous, as he always is, in suggesting the important concepts that he has learned from his study of Marx. What has Marxism learned? How has Marxism developed? Marx died in 1883, and

Lenin in 1924. Fortunately, both left us with our own problems, which, it is to be hoped, we can deal with creatively. There are great human issues which Marxism and Communism and Communist parties and movements have not sufficiently thought about. The reason is that the Marxist-Leninist movement was a polemical effort—grand and colossal. In my opinion, such polemics are philosophically sound, and provide an effective instrument for thinking. But the movement did not think sufficiently about nationalism, for instance. It had a great deal to say about religion, but not nearly as much as that great subject deserves. It did not have enough to say about problems of power because it was out of power—seeking power. When you have power, and Marxism has had power for a relatively short time and in a hostile world, when you have power with people who come out of capitalism, the problems of power —what you should do with it, what its proper scope is, how you guard it—are magnified. There is much more in James Madison than there is in Karl Marx on this enormous problem of power.

The criticisms, the suggestions, the ideas that we get from a Father Quentin Lauer or a Professor Thomas Ogletree, deep Christian but non-Marxist thinkers, we Marxists must listen to with the greatest attention, particularly their questions about human relationships, personal relationships, and about the forms of suffering and doubt. These questions can be enormously instructive for us and will be, as the dialogue continues and, above all, as we live together, in Poland, in Cuba, in Chile, in Italy, and wherever we are forced to.

One final thought. Professor Ogletree's point about

the loss of hope is very perceptive. It is a tremendous danger and a great sign of sickness. It is cynicism. When you become a cynic, you are finished. Cynicism is death. His religious solution is one great way to avoid it. My solution is another. The confidence that he claims to derive from black people can be experienced among other oppressed people, too. I was in Bangladesh before it became Bangladesh. There I saw the horror of racist genocide—the policy of slaughtering 3 million people, mostly women and children. But I saw something else. I saw millions of people rising up to resist—especially the women, to save the children—and to fight back. It depends upon what you look at. When these 3 million people were killed, another 100 million were aroused— and those 100 million won. You can see awful things. You can see napalm being dropped on living flesh, and yet you see people not giving up for twenty-five years. History, in the Marxian sense, is a great source of confidence. It is a great source of confidence in the resistance which is absolutely basic to human history.

I shall end on this note. Marxism speaks of the inevitability of the triumph of socialism, an inevitability due to the action of people. Because needs of masses of people are immutable, the resolution of these needs is inevitable. I view the conflict as you would a prizefight. Suppose you had two prizefighters in a ring, fighting, not for ten rounds or fifteen rounds, but to the end, to death. And suppose you knew that one of the two contestants was immortal. Would you be gambling if you bet on him? Is not his victory inevitable? The demands and the needs of the masses of people are immortal, inexorable. They are always there, napalm or no napalm. Vietnamese have nowhere to go. They don't want to go to Los Angeles. They don't want to go to Hawaii. They want to be in Vietnam long after Nixon. They have been there for 4,000 years of recorded history, and they will remain there. Therefore, they will win—if not this round, the next round. If you are tied to the masses of exploited people, you have a supreme confidence that you cannot lose. I do not need heaven for that. I make my own heaven. My heaven is my partisanship with, and my supreme confidence in, comrades who have faced the supreme test. That's a fact!

These are the thoughts that come to my mind as I consider Professor Ogletree's really splendid essay.

RESPONSE

THOMAS W. OGLETREE

Dr. Aptheker spoke on a number of different levels and raised some very technical problems. He said that religion must always be idealistic. I think not. Let me explain.

I am moved, as all of us are, by the spectacle of human courage. I recall a line from Faulkner which I did not understand when I first read it, but I have thought about it often since. It makes more and more sense to me: "The poor of the earth endure and endure and endure." I cannot say that the poor of the earth are immortal. I can imagine what some are calling ecocatastrophe, an event that would make this planet uninhabitable. I can imagine nuclear holocaust. Under these circumstances, I do not see the poor of the earth enduring and enduring. I do not see how I can be quite as confident of inevitable triumph as Dr. Aptheker seems to be. Yet I do not in any sense wish to say that there is something false or wrong about human courage, wherever it exists and however it is grounded. Actually, human courage is the very stuff of life, the stuff of life which I find to be most interesting and most important.

I suspect Karl Marx himself had both of the levels of hope which I described, though not in ways that were thought through very fully or systematically. He spoke of the ownership and control of the means of production; he spoke of the withering away of the state. These goals sound like a concrete, historical program that has realistic possibilities of future actualization. But Marx also spoke of the humanization of nature and of the naturalization of man. He spoke of Communism. I am continually struck by the connotations the word *Communism* has in Marx's writings. How that word jolts Americans unless they have begun to experience Marx in more positive, critical ways! I learned to associate the word *Communism* with "Red Menace." Many of you did. Perhaps some of you did not. Some of you may have learned the word in other ways first. When Marx talked about Communism, it meant genuine, authentic human community. It meant sensing the oneness of our humanity. It meant being bound together in ties that are far deeper than any of us could dream of.

I am not sure such an image can be called a concrete, historical hope. When Marx talked this way—he didn't very often—he was not talking as a scientist; he was talking as a person who had a sensitive imagination about human possibilities which no science can comprehend. I covet this feature of Marx's thought. I wish it were more fully appreciated by those who call themselves Marxists. Some Marxists attend to such matters. We always have to be specific about which Marxist we have in mind. It is always a question of which Marx you are talking about, and it is the same with Christians. When you say *Christian*, which Christian are you talking about? Are you talking about Martin Luther King? Are you talking about Pope Paul? There is a difference! Are you talking about Father Camilo Torres? Are you talking about Father Dan Berrigan or Father Philip

Berrigan? Are you talking about Billy Graham? We have more than one kind of Christian. One of my favorite Marxists is a man by the name of Ernst Bloch. Bloch says Marxism has a "cold stream" and a "warm stream." We are in the cold stream when we try to be scientific, when we try to analyze what is going on around us.

But we cannot live in cold streams alone. There is passion, imagination and vitality in the human spirit that goes beyond what science can grasp. This stream demands the artist, the poet, the mystic if it is to find adequate expression. I believe the warm stream is very much a part of the human struggle for fulness of life. Again, I feel myself instructed by my encounter with the black revolution. This revolution appears increasingly to be a cultural movement quite as much as it is a political and economic movement. It seeks to draw out the creativity and imagination of a people, to sensitize people more fully in their total being. Such processes are always a part of any struggle that is holistic and human. It is not enough simply to be rational, scientific and political; one needs also to be imaginative, feeling and artistic. The creative, new vision that transforms experience arises precisely in an imagination which shatters scientific analysis. Today we know very well that science can become a "logic of domination." Marcuse has called attention to the fact that people can use science as a means of manipulation and control rather than liberation. In those circumstances, we are most in need of that flowering of the human spirit which breaks through scientific rationality.

When I stress the importance of the religious imagination, it is not because I think there is something

61

inauthentic about the hopes of those who declare themselves atheists. I do not declare anybody's hope inauthentic. Any time human beings are acting with courage
and integrity, I rejoice. I rejoice that something powerful and redemptive is at work among men. But I am also
impressed with the fact that religious imagination can
be one of the things which opens us up to some of the
deeper possibilities of historical existence, possibilities
deeper than those science can disclose to us. Of course,
I cannot speak for everybody in making this claim. Ul-
timately, I can speak only for myself. Yet I suspect others share with me the experience of which I speak. I
find considerable meaning in Marx's notion of the humanization of nature and the naturalization of man. I
believe it can help us get in touch with the kind of
reconciliation all human beings hunger for at the deepest levels of their lives.

I do not know exactly what it means to say that we do
not need anything outside of us. I certainly need food
and air. For many people, the religious imagination expresses a sense of being in touch with the vibrant, thriv-
ing power of the universe, a sense of contact with a
primal energy charging our bodies with life, creating
and re-creating us ever anew. My own religious sensitivities are quite materialistic in a lot of ways. I think my
religious tradition has not appreciated the material
basis of existence fully enough. It has not always taken
seriously the fleshliness that, according to Christian
faith, is part of the divine life itself. My quest is to find
a way to be in touch with this vitality that is mediated
in and through my body, that comes to me in part with
the natural resources I utilize in nourishing my body.

There is power there. A part of what I need as a human being is to be quiet, to be in touch with this grandeur. I cannot always be political. Indeed, sometimes the most creative political acts are not explicitly and directly political at all; they are rather symbolic acts. They are aimed at people's depths, their imaginations, their sensitivities. These things cannot be packaged in a program. Of course, they should not become a replacement for programs of action either! They must rather form the matrix, the ethos, the atmosphere that permeates and conditions political programs.

When I attempt as a theologian to find language for expressing some larger horizon of meaning in which we can all participate, it is to get in touch with that kind of environment and to interpret its meaning for us. I do not believe such meaning has nothing to do with the earth or with my body or with economics; I see it as the informing power of earthly, material movements. It expresses itself in and through such movements. Increasingly, modern religious thinkers find it helpful to speak in this fashion. Pierre Teilhard de Chardin, for example, became influential in part because he was calling for a religion of the earth, a religion which involves the humanization of the biological processes of the world. He saw biological evolution as an analogy for the meaning of our historical struggle. This struggle is not something opposed to the divine life; it is finally the articulation of the divine life. Teilhard's hope was that the earth itself should be overflowing with the divine presence. This kind of understanding does in fact sensitize a lot of people; it gives them an angle of vision on the very concrete problems we face in our world. It does not take people away from the world, but situates them in it with more humane qualities. Everybody may not need that kind of vision. I am not saying they do. We have all kinds of people in our world; each has his own special gift and insight. My concern is to give expression to a dimension of life which is at least a part of the experience of some people, perhaps many.

I do not know how real the hopes are for peace on earth. Many twentieth-century figures who have been deeply influenced by Marx do not share Marx's apparent certainty about the inexorability of the classless society. Franz Fanon, for example, in his magnificent book *The Wretched of the Earth*, acknowledged that he could no longer act as though he were absolutely certain of triumph. He had to find a basis for his hope other than the assurance of victory. We find similar echoes in the writings of other Marxists. Yet people do find hope, and they must find it. We have to draw upon the resources that can give us hope. It is not my task, or anyone else's, to try to shatter bases of hope out of which people are able to live, struggle and survive.

QUESTIONS
ADDRESSED TO
DR. APTHEKER AND
PROFESSOR OGLETREE

Question:

Curiously, the word death is not found in either of your presentations. I wonder how each of you would react if you were confronted by your own death in a particular struggle and came to the realization that you were going to die without attaining some of your most cherished goals?

Aptheker:

Once, when I spoke at the University of North Carolina—it was in 1946 to be exact—I insulted, in my typically gracious manner, the president and faculty of the university, not to mention the entire audience. I stated that their university was not a university because it was segregated. That evening, as I was walking alone to the home of some friends, a group of about six men, armed with clubs, attacked me. I resisted as best I could but without much success. They beat me to the ground. As I lost consciousness, I recall thinking that they were about to kill me. Fortunately, they did not. I don't know why and have not been able to ask them. Now, in regard to my own feelings at the time—I felt mad. I felt that I had to resist. I felt that they were monsters—that what I had said was true, was righteous, was correct, that I couldn't live without saying otherwise, that I had to say what I did, that I would do it again. I thought all those things, and I also thought, "Good God, how stupid I am to walk these streets alone when the sun is down." I shouldn't have done that. I also thought, "Now, how am I going to keep this from my wife." She didn't hear about the attacks so I just explained that we were on tour during the time I was in the hospital and had friends write letters and what-not.

There were a number of other occasions, of course. I was in the army for four years, and in that situation I faced death on numerous occasions. I think—rather I know—that I myself have felt I didn't waste my time here. I did as well as I could. I could have done better in this or that, but I've been tremendously lucky in being able to join the struggle for justice and equal economic opportunity for all human beings. The main issue for me is this struggle. It's right. There's no alternative. That's the way to live. Let me tell you one thing—it sure as hell isn't dull! That's a practical experience. That's the way I felt.

Ogletree:

I do not know exactly how to respond to your question. In some ways it asks for a personal confession, unless you are saying, "You as a theologian certainly should have said something about death. You know atheists don't, but religious people are supposed to be worried about death and to talk about it. Why didn't you 'sock it' to him, because Marxists, you know, don't have anything to say about death that is very creative." I do not know whether such thoughts were behind your question at all. No, I did not talk about death, except indirectly. If you ask me how I deal with it, I must say: not very well. I know people who seem to get a rare kind of excitement out of being in grave danger. Some people do that in what I consider trivial ways, like driving an automobile 195 miles an hour in the Indianapolis "500." That does not "turn me on," yet some people get a rare kind of thrill in such activities and they do not seem to feel they are quite alive unless they are flirting with death. I have also seen people like that in the civil rights movement and in the peace movement. They almost need to die to feel they are authentic human beings. In some ways, I admire such an attitude. It makes you pretty sturdy when you are in the middle of a real crisis. In another way, I do not trust anyone who is like that. In the last analysis, the only person I trust in a tough situation is someone who does not want to die any more than I do.

If you ask me how I respond to such situations, I have to say: I have a hell of a time. When I have thought I had to do something in which death or serious injury was a real possibility, I quickly found a million excuses not to do it. I had to expose my excuses. After the danger passed and I saw that I had made it, I was always relieved, just glad that nothing happened, just hopeful that nothing like that would come up again. Some of you may be heroes. I cannot say that I am particularly heroic about facing death. When I feel that it may be my task to risk my life in order to maintain my integrity, I tend to resent it; I resent the fact that such a task may be laid upon me. I would rather live and simply enjoy my life. At the same time, I think I know something of what Dr. Aptheker meant when he said the glory is in the struggle. When people are part of a movement, they really feel supported by that movement. They are better able to face danger and sacrifice. For many people a religious hope which says that human life has ultimate significance, that finite life will be preserved in the divine life, makes a difference. It gives them more courage and strength to face death. But I also know that some people find it sufficient simply to feel they have lived authentically.

I think sometimes that contemporary philosophy may have overemphasized the importance of death for disclosing the meaning of our humanness, and yet, maybe death is the ultimate question. Maybe it tests more fully than anything else the quality of our commitment, what really counts for us. No one is going to do much about correcting the wrongs of the world without sooner or later having to make some decisions about the meaning of death, without finding some way of taking death into account. How a particular person deals with that fact must be rooted in his or her own personal history.

Aptheker:

I would like to make one more point. I do consider this question in my book, *The Urgency of Marxist-Christian Dialogue*. In that book I take exception to a fellow Marxist writer, Roger Garaudy, who said that, in the face of death, Marxists have nothing to say. I think he is quite wrong, and I said what I think a Marxist ought to say in that book.

Question:

In his response to Dr. Ogletree's remarks about two levels of hope, Professor Aptheker dismissed the second level and placed great emphasis on "the struggle." By so doing he appears to have made "endurance" his criterion of truth. I think that Professor Aptheker has given undue emotional emphasis to "the struggle" and has romanticized the revolutionary hero. Che Guevera was not a romantic hero. He was only a human being. Dr. Aptheker, would you please respond to my observation?

Aptheker:

I did not equate endurance with truth. And I do not believe that endurance equals truth. I did say and do say that the demands of the oppressed are inexorable and that the immortality of the oppressed is plain. Of course, Dr. Ogletree raised, in my view, the one exception to the immortality of these demands—the possibility of nuclear annihilation of our planet. Marx raises this type of issue in the *Manifesto*. He speaks of the inevitability of socialism, given the survival of mankind. At that time, I presume this was pure rhetoric. Nevertheless, it is rather prophetic rhetoric. And so I operate on that assumption. I did not say endurance is truth.

69

Hitler endured for quite a while, but he blew his brains out.

Furthermore, I do not agree with your claim that I glorify "the struggle." If I romanticized it, then I agree with you. But I don't think I did—I don't want to. I am not a romantic; I am a revolutionist. This does not mean that there is no passion, no poetry in Che. He was a revolutionary and also a very passionate person filled with the glory of the struggle. What's wrong with that? It is a glorious thing, and the feeling of comradeship is poetic. It's magnificent. In terms of the movement, I was raised by Bill Foster. Foster told me, "The Communist needs two things (besides everything else that we all know, Herbert). He needs patience and passion." He added, "You find a Communist that doesn't have passion—that's an F. B. I. agent." This is why I am dedicated to the struggle. It is a glorious thing. Therefore, get in it. That's when you will begin to live. What's wrong with that?

Question:

Religions present themselves as ideal solutions to human problems. However, in practice they often become part of the problem. There have been many times in human history when religion has been used by people in power to maintain the *status quo* or justify an unjust or oppressive system. For example, a noted theologian once remarked that the most segregated hour in America is from 11:00 a.m. to 12:00 noon on Sunday. And Marx claimed that religion is the opiate of the people. How do each of you deal with this problem?

70

Ogletree:

I am impressed with the fact that we constantly tend to profane and to domesticate all powerful and creative expressions of understanding in human history. What bursts into human experience as a challenge to the existing order gets turned into a justification for special privilege. I do not think Christianity is unique in this process. I believe Christianity is an explosive, radical perspective on life. Yet when we encounter something explosive and radical which is threatening to us, we have to do something to get rid of the threat. The best way to get rid of such a threat is to identify with it, domesticate it, routinize it. I believe this happens in Marxism, too. Marxism is an explosive, critical perspective. Marx began the *Manifesto* by speaking of a specter haunting Europe. Everybody trembles before Communism, he noted. Something creative and powerful was going on. Yet that same explosive, critical perspective can be used to justify Stalinist oppression or the bureaucratic mentality of the German Democratic Republic (East Germany). As Dr. Aptheker pointed out, Marxism includes within itself a critical perspective, and if it is true to itself, it will remain critical. Likewise, the Judeo-Christian tradition includes within itself a prophetic perspective, but that does not mean that the prophetic perspective is always effective. I am increasingly convinced—in this sense I am a materialist—that the prophetic perspective is most effectively kept alive among people who are oppressed. The privileged can never hear the prophetic word very easily. This is always the way it is: criticism comes from those who experience in their own being that which is broken in the present order of things, the contradictions of the existing situation. The oppressed are the ones who can see and intuitively know the prophetic power of a religious heritage or the critical power of Marxism. In short, though what you say is true, you have identified an *inherent* human problem, not a distinctive failing of Christianity. It is misleading to say Christianity has been around 2,000 years and yet has not solved all human problems. Within certain particular situations, Christianity has, in fact, created very liberating, human environments. New problems came, however, and it continually adjusted itself to an established order. Frankly, I do not believe that 2,000 years of Marxism will bring in a classless society—or a kingdom of freedom. We may find that it, too, increasingly becomes for some people a legitimation of privilege and power—for example, of an elite in the Kremlin. I think this is an inherent human problem. I think it is a problem Marxism has. I think it is a problem Christianity has. It would be a mistake for a Marxist to want to defend everything that calls itself Marxism. The critical cutting edge is lost when that is attempted. I also think it is a mistake for a Christian to call everything prophetic that genuflects.

Aptheker:

I find no problem with much of what Professor Ogletree said. Yet I want to add a few thoughts to his response. The most important changes in our society must come decisively from the people who are religious. I do

72

not think that the criticism can be effective from those who are not. And I think that one of the great facts at this time in human history is the increasing crisis in all institutional churches. Now that crisis comes, in my opinion, from the general crisis of capitalism and imperialism. It reflects itself in philosophical and organizational and institutional and hierarchical problems, and it also reflects itself in human beings—in the fact that thousands of priests are leaving the Roman Catholic Church. They are not losing their religiosity. They are becoming critical of the institution to the point that they finally conclude that they cannot remain in it but must fight for its alteration from the outside. But they have not given up. And the prophetic dimension is a decisive dimension of all religions, not least of all the Christian. I tried to point to this crisis very briefly in my paper. I cited the Berrigans and individuals in Catonsville, Chile and Northern Italy. These are people within the church who are very devoted to it. I also want to remind you that the Christian tradition has produced Martin Luther King, Jr. and A. J. Muste—great Christians and tremendously effective human beings, fighters within their own churches for revision. They are a part of the reality of their religious traditions. Such activity is going on everywhere, including Judaism and Islam. There is a left and a right in Islam, and the recent setback in Pakistan was a tremendous blow to the worst elements in that religious community.

One final remark. Marx did not say religion is the opiate of the people. If you quote Marx in that context, it is like claiming that Jesus said, "Go and sin!" He said this. However, you need to complete the sentence. Jesus said, "Go and sin no more." It's almost as incorrect to quote Marx in such a manner. Actually, you must read the essay, or at least the paragraph, in which this sentence is found. Marx states that religion is the spirit of a spiritless world, religion is the perfume of a world that stinks, religion is the source of strength in a world that crushes people, religion is the opiate. That is the sense of his meaning. To vulgarize it so that Marx becomes a village atheist, a nut, or a devotee of Robert Ingersoll—without any more wisdom than that—is to misrepresent him. That's all right for the late J. Edgar Hoover, but it is not all right for any serious discussion of Marxism on religion.

Question:

I contend that Professor Ogletree has been more sympathetic towards the basic dogmas of Marx than the basic beliefs of Christianity. Therefore, I allege that a Christian-Marxist dialogue has not transpired. In fact, this situation reveals how it is impossible for a fair dialogue to be conducted between Christians and Marxists.

Also, I want to challenge Dr. Aptheker's claim that he is not a religious person. He mentioned God at least four different times. He shows a great religious fervor in his devotion to Marxism. However, I feel he only worships himself. Thus he lives according to his own religion, not a transcendent one.

Ogletree:

It appears as though you have Christianity nicely packaged. I do not believe I was speaking of Marxist dogma. The word dogma is a tricky word to use. I understood myself as identifying *one very important contribution* that Marx makes to our approach to concrete problems of social existence. I wanted to argue that the concern for such things comes out of fundamental features of Christian faith, at least for me. I wanted to argue that no one can take seriously a Christian proclamation of liberation for the oppressed, the setting at liberty of those who are in prison, the recovery of sight for the blind, deliverance for the poor—that no one can take seriously that kind of gospel—and at the same time pay no attention to how one addresses those problems in a concrete way. When Christianity pursues such a course, it really does become an "idealism," and its images, its special language, do not make any difference in terms of the way we face concrete problems. I am saying that it is precisely out of a concern for this fundamental theme of Christian faith, this central motif— certainly I haven't elaborated the whole range of Christian thought—that I have turned to Marxism. I centered on certain crucial issues related to the motif of hope. I am saying that my use of Marxism is itself informed by a certain understanding of Christian faith. My Christian perspective leads me to an engagement with Marx and the Marxist movement. That is all I am saying.

Aptheker:

The respondent alleges that I employed the word God four times. So what? I can use any word I wish. And, of course, in common speech one speaks of God. Hence the observation is an absurd remark. Second, I am not God, and, unlike the respondent, I do not know God. He does. He's very confident. That is fine. But I am not God. I am convinced, however, that man made God. This is my belief. I believe man made the image, and I believe that God is in man's image. Man makes God. This is my belief. And to twist this in a way that could only have been intended—unless the respondent is indeed moronic—to prove that Aptheker says that he is God is, of course, again absurd. This kind of disgusting conduct has no place, either in a university or in a serious effort at dialogue between Marxists and Christians.

LATIN AMERICA–
WHERE THE DIALOGUE
BECOMES PRAXIS

SHEPHERD BLISS

The excellent essays by Christian theologian Thomas Ogletree and Marxist theoretician Herbert Aptheker and the ensuing dialogue evoke contrasting images from my experiences in Latin America: hope/liberation, dialogue/praxis, books/streets, conventional/revolutionary, North Atlantic/Latin America. These images indicate the differences between the more traditional Christian-Marxist dialogue of Aptheker and Ogletree and the praxis of liberation emerging from the streets, jungles and mountains of Latin America.

Praxis is the word which best characterizes what is happening among Christians and Marxists in Latin America. Praxis is a Marxist term which is becoming more common among Christians because of the efforts of intellectual workers such as exiled Brazilian Paulo Freire. It refers to that practical functioning which is the unity of thought and action. Praxis is reflected behavior revealed historically. A fundamental commonality of Marxism and Christianity is that they both take history seriously, affirming that people are shaped by their historical reality.

The Christian-Marxist dialogue which began in the First World in the early 1960's and may have made significant contributions to human knowledge and understanding differs from what has been emerging among Christians and Marxists in Latin America. The objective conditions of exploitation in Latin America demand an urgency to overcome the causes of this deprivation. In such a situation, concrete action takes priority over abstract talk.

A comparison of the concerns of Ogletree and Aptheker to the theology taught in U.S. seminaries in the 1960's and 1970's makes me grateful to these two men. However, when I compare their thoughts and actions to those of theologians such as Peruvian Gustavo Gutierrez, Brazilian Hugo Assman, and Uruguayan Juan Luis Segundo, I conclude that such Latin Americans who utilize Marxist science to understand society speak more directly to our historical reality. While most North Atlantic theologians sit comfortably in seminary classrooms, Latin American Christians acting on their theology of liberation have been jailed, physically tortured, exiled and even killed for their militant expressions of Christian faith applied to social injustices.

Dr. Ogletree was one of the rare seminary professors in the entire city of Chicago, where I was a seminarian in the late 1960's, whose work showed even an awareness of the comprehensive crisis occurring in the U.S. and throughout the world. I drew inspiration from the *Openings for Marxist-Christian Dialogue* which he edited in 1968. During this time I became aware of the dedicated work of Dr. Aptheker as the North American Marxist who has made the greatest contribution to this dialogue. The symposium on *Marxism and Christianity* which he edited in 1968 and his subsequent *The Ur-*

gency of Marxist-Christian Dialogue have already become classics in the field.

These works appeared in the historical context of a decade full of U. S. wars and ventures into the Third World, domestic racism, continued sexism, and the extended growth of international capitalism. Rather than indict these oppressions and indicate strategies for struggle in the Exodus-Resurrection spirit, the various theologies taught in seminaries more often function to domesticate human struggles. Theologians at the best universities and Christians well placed in the corporate state were themselves too comfortable to recall the Exodus-Resurrection demand for the liberation of all peoples. They were isolated, unable to hear the cries. The rewards of capitalism became too tempting—such as continued money from the Rockefeller family for religious *institutions*. Even the "political theology" of Germans such as Metz and Moltmann does not sufficiently reveal the causes of the imbalances in society nor indicate strategies to redeem our dying culture.

Latin American Theology

Fortunately for my own theological growth, I discovered, while still in seminary, theologians who were not committed to advocating the *status quo* and benefiting from it with high salaries, book royalties, and status positions. The. first major work by a Latin American theologian of liberation to appear in English, only as recently as 1969, was that of Brazilian Rubem Alves, who criticizes obsolete theological paradigms which prevent conceptual breakthroughs. Though it became immediately clear to me that Latin American theologians were speaking to the real issues of our day, there were no seminary professors to help me with this work. They preferred that I learn German rather than Spanish to do my work; I became aware of a subtle institutional channeling.

Ogletree's and Aptheker's commonalities as North Americans and as relative traditionalists within their respective fields are as salient as are their differences based on their respective Christian and Marxist traditions. The situation is different in Latin America. Both Christians and Marxists find existing paradigms insufficient. Latin Americans are breaking new ground. Though both Christianity and Marxism are international, their historical expressions are conditioned by cultural, national, and continental variables. I am not proposing a continental chauvinism or the pre-eminence of either Latin American Christianity or Marxism. Rather, my contention is that the contemporary Latin American experience offers dialectical critiques of both twentieth-century Marxism and Christianity, especially in their North Atlantic forms. A deeply human and spiritual *grito* (cry) for justice has been detonated out of the very oppression and powerlessness of the Third World.

Ogletree and Aptheker were involved in a *dialogue* about *hope*. The basic structure of this conversation was obviously determined by North American Christians. Both *dialogue* and *hope* are common and comfortable to readers of contemporary theology, which has charged these words with specific meanings. In contrast, Latin American Christians commonly talk about other issues—dependence, dialectics, colonialism, subversion. These differences are important: dialogues tend to be consensual interchanges in which the truth is supposed to be somewhere in the middle, whereas the dialectic leads to a synthesis which is the result of a conflict between a thesis and antithesis. Aptheker points to the importance of this ongoing dialectic when he admits that "Marxism holds forth no final solution." Marxism is a process; whenever it is reduced to stasis, as by some political sects in the U. S. (e.g., National Caucus of Labor Committees or Spartacist League), we cannot call this Marxism.

Latin Americans do not emphasize Christian-Marxist *dialogue*, rather Christian-Marxist *praxis*. Talk is not so important as working together to eliminate oppression and exploitation and facilitate liberation and freedom. If dialogue helps in this process, all power to it. However, Protestant Rubem Alves describes how religious language often functions to solve problems in the abstract rather than in reality. Religious people often feel as if the mere act of articulating a problem were sufficient, freeing them from the necessity to solve it. Unlike Europe, in Latin America a sophisticated Christian-Marxist dialogue does not exist; yet Christians and Marxists know each other and often work together intimately.

While North American theologians frequently continue to deal with abstractions almost as obscure as counting angels on the head of a pin, Latin American theologians have to deal with the very substance of life and threats to survival. While Christianity in the North Atlantic becomes more abstract and isolated from the

81

lives of the masses, in Latin America the faith continues to be a common concern of the various *pueblos* (peoples). For example, instead of living amidst the security of a well-furnished rectory, Gonzalo Arroyo lives in a *poblacion* (shanty-town) on the outskirts of Santiago de Chile, where he shares a life of minimal material benefits with his *pueblo*. Bolivian Nestor Paz felt the contradiction of the advantages of the seminary where he was studying and the meagerness of his *pueblo*. He left for the mountains to live and struggle. Nestor Paz's tragic death was not unlike that of many Bolivians; he apparently starved to death when he could find no more berries or roots. Latin American theology emerges more from these objective conditions than from book-reading and seminary-teaching. Its Marxism has a similar immediacy.

Hope

Now I shall turn to the interesting conversation about "hope" in the Ogletree-Aptheker dialogue. Both agree that it has something to do with a subject which has great popularity among North Atlantic philosophers and theologians these days. North American Christians are familiar with "hope, faith, and charity," both from the Bible and from civil religion as sung by cowboy Roy Rogers. But how is it that hope has come, recently, to take such prominence over even faith and love? European theologians such as Metz and Moltmann have put this concept in vogue. German Marxist Ernst Bloch, whom Ogletree mentions and whom theologians are now reading, also uses it frequently. Jacques Ellul, whom the Berrigan brothers and others are turning to these days, recently published a book with *hope* in the title. Even humanist socialist Erich Fromm has written a book about theology and hope.

From a Latin American perspective, this emphasis on hope serves more to conceal essential problematics than reveal our historical problems so that we can begin to deal with them. There is a sense in which this "hope" is a renaming of the capacity of Christianity to hold out for future better things rather than struggle within history. The language about hope has the danger of encouraging us to solve our problems in the abstract rather than with liberating praxis. Hope language does not provide an understanding of our reality, a pedagogy, within which we can engage in redeeming actions.

Latin Americans every day voice *esperanza* (hope), but contemporary Latin American theologians seek to place *liberacion* more on the agenda. The solution for hopelessness is not necessarily talk about hope; it is rather understandings and strategies which result in behavior which initiates the awakening (*concientizacion*) of the struggles which overcome hopelessness. The direct translation of the Spanish version of Rubem Alves' first book would be "Religion: Opiate or Instrument of Liberation?" Yet the English version bears the title "A Theology of Human Hope." It is a serious mistake to confuse liberation and hope and think they are the same thing. Dr. Alves told me that he did not suggest or choose the English title. His American editors made the decision.

Hope, though certainly not without merit, operates at a high level of abstraction. In contrast, liberation is a process, a movement, a praxis, a doing. (One form of U. S. cultural imperialism is the frequency with which U. S. editors alter titles and meanings in their translations. The work of guerrilla-priest Camilo Torres has been greatly damaged by translations. Herder and Herder changed the original title of his essay "Revolution: Christian Imperative" to "The Christian Apostolate and Economic Planning"!!)

My Christian brother Ogletree talks about two levels of Christian hope—"the ultimate religious hope and the concrete, historical hope." My Marxist comrade Aptheker, though he does not deal as directly with hope, talks about "the very great practical usefulness of utopianism." He then presents a "detailed and specific program" toward which he aspires. He concludes that our mutual hope as humans consists in our common resistance to exploitation. Many Latin American Christians and Marxists would certainly agree with these observations on hope. But the expressions of hope by Latin Americans have an immediacy and concreteness I find lacking in Ogletree, Aptheker, and others in the North Atlantic world. For example, members of the Puerto Rican Socialist Party (who count among its sympathizers Catholic Bishop Antulio Parilla-Bonilla) have asserted to me that the only true basis of hope is an organized, mobilized people willing to struggle for its liberation. I think they are correct.

Much of the talk about hope—not so much by Ogletree and Aptheker as by Europeans—leaves Latin Americans cold. Such talk remains too abstract, eschatological, and future-oriented; it does not seem to emerge from or relate directly to the daily lives of the people. If theology is for more than a small elite, it must be conceived and written in modes distinct from those typical in the North Atlantic countries. What, after all, should we Christians expect from our theologians? This is a question with which Marxists can help us. We justifiably can demand that our theologians provide us with language and symbols adequate to the expression of the problems and faith of our historical time. All probably would agree with this statement. We must also expect faithful actions and lives from these theologians. There are U. S. theologians, for example, whose praxis is to make lots of money and live in big mansions; we must be critical of them, remembering that "it is easier for a camel to go through the eye of a needle than for a rich man to enter the kingdom of God." (Matthew 19:24) We must hold up the example of Chilean Christians, such as Gonzalo Arroyo, who lives among the people, developing his theology there. Theologians who make lots of money, live in big houses and drive big cars tend to write in abstractions and to be accountable to people with money; theologians who live among the people tend to write more concretely and to be accountable to the people. My seminary professors dismissed the theology which is emerging from the concrete realities of Latin America as "mere political pamphleteering." It is true that Latin American theology does not have all the niceties and refined language of North Atlantic theology. But Third World theologies of liberation seem more Biblical and faithful, at least to pre-Constantine Christianity, than those theologies which prevail in the North Atlantic nations.

The opposite of hope is cynicism and pessimism. Both

are rampant these days. When their anti-war efforts were not quickly successful, many liberals and New Left radicals seem to have abandoned the struggle. There were a variety of reasons for their action. They lacked an ideology to carry them through. They were too issue- and crisis-oriented. They became tired and burned out. Yet Christians and Marxists realize, each from their own tradition, that there is no action of theirs which can bring about the necessary permanent change. Christian teaching emphasizes that the "Kingdom of God" is not brought in by any individual action. Marxist teaching also stresses that the struggle is a life-long process, rather than an event.

Latin American Marxists and Christians are aware of and practice these tenets of their respective faiths. The five months I spent in Chile in 1971 spurred my personal hope, as I witnessed Christians and Marxists working together toward the common creation of a more just society without surrendering to cynicism and pessimism when they encounter difficulties and reversals. When Fidel Castro visited the Chilean people for a month in 1971, his enthusiasm and humanity were contagious. He embodied much of the "New Man" of which both St. Paul and "Che" Guevara speak. I attended a liturgical service in Chile convened by "Christians for Socialism," the group mentioned by Aptheker. It occurred outside one of the local offices of the Communist Party. This mass, attended by Christian and Marxist revolutionaries alike, commemorated the assassination of the Brazilian resistance leader Carlos Lamarca. We felt comfortable, Christian and Communist, even when we gathered together in the church building. Our unity was deeper than any "ism."

Class Struggle

Without attacking the problem directly, both Ogletree and Aptheker allude to one of the major problems which divides Christians and Marxists: class struggle. Christians have difficulty dealing with conflict of any sort. Most of them are dominated by a vague feeling that somehow all humans should cooperate and get along. Yet the Bible itself is an intense expression of struggle. However, since the church joined the state at Constantinople in the third century, only a remnant community has continued with the Biblical mandate to "preach liberation to the captives." (John 4:18) A major role of the church during the period of capitalist development has been to teach the sanctity of the established order and authority. This acceptance has been masked over by doctrines of reconciliation.

Christians seem often able to accept the factual observation that capitalist society is divided into two distinct classes, the one rich and the other systematically poor, and that these rich oppress these poor. But many Christians define the "Christian response" to this situation to be philanthropy, the toleration of institutional violence, and the eventuality of the miraculous reconciliation of these two naturally antagonistic classes. It is difficult for Christians to accept the fact that the resolution of class divisions comes through class struggle.

Another major problem, in addition to the pacifying

87

effect of the doctrine of reconciliation-without-struggle, is caused by the fact that many Christians line up on the wrong side of the struggle. They integrate themselves into the dominant class. There is a great involvement in American society of wealthy families and their monies within the major institutions—the army, the government, corporations, banks, universities, and the church. The Rockefeller family, for example, has been a major exploiter of workers for years. Though John D. Rockefeller gave the order to massacre miners at Ludlow, Colorado, in 1914, he also founded the divinity school from which I was graduated, the University of Chicago. With an instinct to protect this blood money, another Rockefeller gave the order in 1971 for triggers to be pulled at Attica—over forty bodies lay dead. Yet this same Rockefeller family continues to give heavily to religious institutions. There is a unity of behavior in killing black prisoners at Attica and endowing religious institutions; both actions, each in its own way, repress class struggle. As Carl Braden of the Southern Conference Education Fund (which is one of the few U. S. groups which seem to have historically united Christians and Marxists in common work) pointed out on Easter, 1972, at the Harrisburg Trial of the Berrigan brothers, "This system tries to get you one way or the other—by co-opting you, by buying you off, by beating you up, by jailing you, or finally by killing you."

Latin American Christians demand that North American Christians scrutinize their society, pose fundamental questions, and develop strategies for comprehensive structural change. Fortunately, not all U. S. Christians have been domesticated by either the benefits of the dominant class or an innocent ideology of reconciliation. When Marx was writing in the mid-1800's, "Christian Socialists" began to appear in England. Right before the turn of the century, they became more numerous in the U.S., particularly around Boston. One of their chief spokespersons was the Rev. W. Dwight Porter Bliss, editor of the *Dawn*, who wrote the following in 1890:

> Have a care, then, men of money. Your money is losing its power. Friend Astor, with your $150 million, you will not always own New York City. Trinity Church, with your $150 million, you may learn some day that the Church as well as man may be in danger of gaining the whole world and losing its own soul. C. Vanderbilt, W. K. Vanderbilt, Jay Gould, J. D. Rockefeller, with your $100 million each, not always shall you own enough to feed the unfed in all the country.

Perhaps it is only idle speculation, but I feel strongly that the course of history would have been quite different if these Christian Socialists who preached the Biblical mandate of liberation had been followed seriously. Maybe those millions of Vietnamese would not have died. Each time struggle emerges actively in the U. S.— such as in the late nineteenth century and again in the 1930's—it is brutally suppressed. Yet Christians are called to side with the oppressed and poor (labor) in their struggle against domination by the rich (capital).

Marxism asserts that there is an inherent contradiction between capital and labor, i.e., between capitalists

89

and workers, between rich and poor. The fundamental problem is a structural one, but there are individuals and families who perpetuate these oppressive structures who will never willingly give up their power and privilege. The resolution to this dilemma cannot be an innocent, wishful reconciliation, as some Christians would assert. Such reconciliation is impossible when one class has all the power. A more appropriate solution is humane, informed, disciplined, selected expressions of class struggle—the effect of which would be the destruction of the class basis of the current society, a resultant classless society, and reconciliation. There can be no peace without justice, no reconciliation without struggle. This, I would assert, is "the peace which passes all understanding".

Latin American Christianity can help us deal with this question of class struggle, a question which has not been dealt with sufficiently by most North Atlantic participants in the Christian-Marxist dialogue. I am reminded of the observation of exiled Bolivian theologian Hugo Assman, recorded in the ISAL (Church and Society in Latin America group) publication, *Oppression-Liberation: Challenge to Christians* (not yet in English): "The incipient dialogue between Christians and Marxists, as it has been attempted in the rich world, appears to avoid direct confrontation with the real challenges of the historical moment."

Christianity mandates us to choose love always, which seems antithetical to class struggle. The Third World priests in Argentina, confronted often with this dilemma, have laid the foundation for understanding how love and class struggle are related:

90

To live the commandment of love involves a political position, whether one likes it or not. Today one cannot follow the Gospel without political activity. It is impossible that one live responsibly without being concerned with the organization of society.

Father Camilo Torres of Colombia had this love, for which he was assassinated by the military. He elaborates on what the Argentine priests say as follows:

Love of the neighbor must be efficacious. In the actual circumstances of Latin America it is necessary to favor the seizure of power by the majority so that they can realize reforms for the common good. This is called "revolution"; if it is necessary for the realization of neighbor, then a Christian ought to be a revolutionary.

Latin American theologians have rejected most North Atlantic theology because it does not speak to their reality, as Uruguayan Juan Luis Segundo, S. J., pointed out in the 1973 Dudleian Lecture given at Harvard Divinity School. However, there is one Spanish theologian, Giulio Girardi, whose writings on love and class struggle are read throughout Latin America. At a talk in Spain in 1969 he developed his basic thesis at great length, from which I have excerpted the following:

We must see the difference between struggle and hatred. We need a new way to interpret the demands of love. The Gospel bids us to love our enemies; it does not tell us not to have enemies, or not to combat them. There is no incompatibility between love and class struggle. A serious Christian love implies dedicating oneself to the liberation of the oppressed and the global transformation of the system that "manufactures" the poor. It calls for struggling against the inevitable resistance from all the forces bent on preserving their comfortable status quo. The privileged class never relinquishes its position of power spontaneously, only when it loses the struggle.

Later on in the same talk he asserted:

Not only does love not exclude class struggle, it requires it. One cannot love the poor without lining up with them in their struggle for liberation. The class struggle is becoming, for the new Christian conscience, an imperative inseparable from the commandment of love. Christian love has a new meaning: not a static, but a dynamic, transforming love, which impels us not only to see man as he is, but to create a "New Man"—not an individualistic, but a community man, i.e., with the mission of creating a new world that will be combative and militant, consequently will be "for all."

Latin American Challenges to Orthodoxy and Reformism

Ogletree does not represent the institutional church in his views on Marxism; nor does Aptheker represent the traditional view of Communist parties on Christianity. Yet neither present a revolutionary option; both want their respective institutions to become more dialogical. Latin Americans such as Camilo Torres and Nestor Paz present another option for living out one's Christian faith in a praxis striving to develop a socialist society. Torres and Paz present a challenge to both orthodox and reform-minded Christians.

So, too, the Cuban Revolution challenges Marxists

throughout the world. Fidel Castro's adherence to moral incentives rather than material incentives in economics shocked his Eastern European advisors. Fidel's entire political and personal style, so deeply Latin American, is a further challenge to orthodox Marxism. This became clear when Fidel visited Chile in 1971 and Eastern Europe in 1973. Cardinal Raul Silva y Henriquez of Chile presented Fidel a Bible with his name engraved on it. Fidel's response: "I accept this book with great pleasure, knowing it is one of the great books in the world. It contains many correct teachings." He then proceeded to recite a couple of parables: the fish and loaves being multiplied to feed the many, and workers arriving at different hours and yet receiving the same wages. He concluded that both of these parables of Jesus were "good Communist teaching." While in Chile, Fidel criticized the church as an institution used by the dominant class to pacify people. He did not criticize the Christian faith itself or its adherents. Churches and seminaries still exist in Cuba. However, they are no longer in league with the state, as churches throughout the world are, to mystify the people and domesticate their righteous struggle.

Christians in Cuba and throughout Latin America recall the Exodus as the historical basis of socialism. The Hebrew people were the first to understand that history is linear and not cyclical and repetitive. This insight helped them discover that they could make history. They did so by liberating themselves from enslavement to the Egyptians. Marxists might call this Biblical episode the primordial experience of "armed struggle." Though not peaceful, pleasant, or reconciling, in the end, this militantly liberating process brought all these benefits and more.

So, too, the Resurrection is a revolutionary experience of "New Life," a loud "no" to the old, which Marxists call a "negation of the negative," and a hopeful "yes" to the future. Christians championed these two symbols of struggle—Exodus and Resurrection—until the third century, when the church joined the state at Constantinople. Only a remnant body, often outside the institution, has remained to preach the liberation which Luke recalls so clearly in 4:18: "He has sent me to proclaim release to the captives, and recovering of sight to the blind, to set at liberty those who are oppressed."

In pursuit of this Christian mandate of liberation, in Romans 8 St. Paul argues: ". . . the sufferings of this present time are not worth comparing with the glory that is to be revealed to us . . . the whole creation has been groaning in travail until now; and not only the creation, but we ourselves."

There is pain but such pain lies in the very nature of expectation and demands our further struggle. Some Christians would interpret these and other such Biblical passages as having to do with another world, up in the sky or somehow beyond. But it seems clear to me that they are talking about this world—including the world in which we live and are called to herald the sons and daughters of our Lord by our integration into processes of liberation.

During the last third of the twentieth century, much of the groaning, remnant community of faithful Christians dwells in Latin America. This community challenges both Christians and Marxists to live out their principles. The problem is not whether we are Christians or Marxists, but whether—as Christians, Marxists, or whatever—our lives point beyond themselves and are united with others struggling for justice. In this struggle Christianity and Marxism can be complementary, though there are sell-outs (*vendidos*) in both camps. Apart, or even in collaboration, neither is sufficient, though both can assist us in the living-together-as-humans process. I see Marxism and Christianity as two expressions, neither complete, of a deeper truth. It is dangerous to accept either as *the* Way. Both, and more, point toward that redeemed world to which each of us aspires. To exchange one dogmatism for another is unproductive. Both Christianity and Marxism can be liberating; both have been liberating for me personally. But the institutions of both have often become oppressive. At a 1972 conference in Quebec (see below) the final theological document asserted the following:

> Both the Christians and Marxists have sometimes succumbed to a totalitarian and static concept of their social role, but this is a falsification of Christianity and of Marxism. In many ways Marxism is an expression, in modern, secular scientific terms, of the tradition of Christian hope and Christian judgment against evil.

There is a danger among both Christians and Marxists in their tendency to absolutize whatever effective forms—such as political parties and religious denominations—they develop. These forms then become institutionalized and oppressive. Both among Christians and Marxists there are two contrary thrusts; one we might call *Constantine* because of its establishment character, and the other *revolutionary* because of its liberating character.

During the last decade Latin American Christians, both those sympathetic to Marxism and others, have begun to challenge orthodox Christians. This has become most obvious at international gatherings. Latin American Catholics, such as Bishop Sergio Mendez Arceo of Cuernavaca, Mexico, raised crucial questions at Vatican II in the early 1960's. In its activities at Geneva and throughout the world, the World Council of Churches has also been a forum for Latin American theologians of liberation. Much of this militant energy was focused and expressed in 1968 at the Second Latin American Bishops Conference in Medellin, Colombia. At this conference even the bishops uttered a clear cry for liberation. Since this conference there have emerged a number of religious forces throughout Latin America demanding liberation—Golconda in Colombia, ONIS in Peru, Christians for Socialism in Chile, Third World Priests in Argentina, and the continental-wide activities of ISAL, particularly in Bolivia, Uruguay, and Ecuador. Most of these groups use Marxism as a science to understand dependence and imperialism.

I have attended several meetings of U. S., European, and Latin American Christians in which the differences between North Atlantic and Latin American Christians were articulated quite clearly. Two such meetings stand out in my mind and perhaps clarify Latin American Christianity and its affinity to Marxism. In July of 1971 the World Council of Christian Education met near Lima, Peru. Though those from the North Atlantic countries would have been more comfortable with the traditional talks on "ecumenism" and "hope," usually conducted at such conferences, Latin Americans struck a new tone with their discussions of "dependence," "imperialism," and "liberation." In October of 1972 the Second International Assembly of Christians in Solidarity with the Indo-Chinese People met in Quebec. Rather than getting lost in piety, Puerto Rican Bishop Antulio Parilla Bonilla led a worship service in which he openly called for the total victory of the heroic Vietnamese people over their U. S. aggressors. During the conference Gonzalo Arroyo spoke words which articulate my point: "We must be critical of an innocent Christian theology which conceals the Biblical message of liberation. We must choose a theology thoroughly dedicated to the people and their struggles." In such international gatherings Latin American Christians have often been a challenge to various Christian orthodoxies.

I recall the words of a Bishop of my own communion, Argentine Federico Pagura, who posed the following question in a recent Methodist publication in the U. S." "Why are North Americans so afraid of words like 'socialism' and 'revolution'?" The main reason is that North Americans are a part of the problem, not the solution. We know that much of the "revolution" will be against us. The task of integrating ourselves into processes of liberation as North American residents in what Che Guevara calls "the belly of the monster," will not be an easy one. Yet one Latin American after another has told me that the greatest struggle is within the U. S.; it is here, more than anywhere else, where Christians must assume their task of "liberating the captives." For it is here in the U. S. that the structures of captivity are built.

Another reason for our fear of "socialism" and "revolution," other than our privileges as North Americans, is the strong anti-communist campaign in this country. Churches have even been used to launch these attacks. Yet Christians in these very churches, if they would recall the Exodus and Resurrection, would join Marxists in our common struggle against domination by a powerful ruling elite.

Crystallization

Neither Marxism nor Christianity are monolithic; there are many expressions of both. Ogletree points out that "we have more than one kind of Christian"; Marxism also takes many forms. Radical Christians are likely to discover that they have more in common with radical Marxists than with reactionary Christians. Though both Marxism and Christianity propose comprehensive worldviews, many Christians do not accept the totality of these respective views. Marxism includes, among other things, philosophy, science, economics, political organization, and psychology. Consequently, one can employ the Marxist dialectical method of scientific inquiry and not necessarily agree with all of its philosophical tenets.

Marxism and Christianity are at opposite poles to some persons. Even those Christians sympathetic to Marxism sometimes feel they cannot identify themselves as "Marxists." Ogletree, for example, felt the need to say the following: "I cannot call myself a Marxist. I think there is something a little bit odd about such a designation. I am not even sure Marx would consider himself a Marxist. . . ." Perhaps so, but true also of "Christian." Would Christ have called himself a "Christian"? This oddness of which Ogletree speaks does not prevail in Latin America. In Chile, for example, it is possible for members of the Communist Party to go to mass every Sunday morning and see no inherent contradiction. I was glad that Dr. Aptheker mentioned the "Christians for Socialism" conference attended by some 400 delegates from nearly two dozen countries in 1972 in Chile. At this conference there were people who consider themselves both "socialist" and "Christian." As an ordained Methodist minister, I also feel myself to be a socialist—in that I understand society as divided between capital and labor (rich and poor), that the means of production should be owned by organized workers rather than by an elite, and that class struggle is consistent with the love mandate.

As a Christian socialist, then, my criticism of fellow Marxists needs to be that they are not adequately pursuing their Marxist agenda, not that they do not believe in the Lord Jesus Christ. I might also raise the issue that they should consider the importance of my concern with transcendence, but never in a proselytizing manner. As a Christian socialist, my criticism of Christians needs to be, primarily, that they do not seem to adhere adequately to the driving Biblical symbols of the Exodus and the Resurrection. I might also point out that our tradition does not adequately assess certain realities, particularly economic ones. But once again, it is on our basic tenets that my discussion with Christians proceeds, bringing in analysis which our tradition lacks.

Ogletree mentions that "when Marx talked about Communism, it meant genuine, authentic community." Therein is an essential commonality between Marxism and Christianity—humans trying to live together equally. We North American citizens of this republic need to examine, especially in light of Watergate, whether our form of government adequately facilitates democracy and this living together. Formal democracy was born in Greece; with U. S. support fascism now dominates Greece. In another allegedly democratic republic supported by the U. S., Brazil, even the word "community" is officially outlawed. Its mere mention in a song is punishable by physical torture. If we were to reorganize the U. S.'s economy and government on a Marxian rather than capitalist basis, it would not look like Russia, China, Cuba, or Chile. Our historical tradition is distinct, as is each of the different republics of Latin America. Latin Americans always tell me that the most Christian thing North Americans can do for them is to struggle within the U. S. to reform their own country and to stop oppressing the world with the growth of their international capitalism. They remind me of Tolstoi's famous words:

> I sit on a man's back, choking him and making him carry me, and yet assure myself and others that I am very, very sorry for him and wish to lighten his load by all possible means—except by getting off his back.

My basic argument, then, has been that we must distinguish between dialogue as the usual North Atlantic intellectual relationship between Marxism and Christianity and praxis as the working relationship between the two which the immediacy of the Latin American situation demands. Whereas dialogue leads us to a mutual concern with hope, praxis leads us to tactical and strategic considerations of processes of human liberation. Regardless of the labels we employ—workers and intellectuals, Christians and Marxists—those of us who are committed to the struggle for social justice must unite.

SUGGESTIONS FOR FURTHER READING

S. A. Garcia and C. R. Calle (eds.), *Camilo Torres: Priest and Revolutionary*. London: Sheed and Ward, 1968.

Regis Debray, *The Chilean Revolution*. New York: Random House, 1971.

Gustavo Gutierrez, *A Theology of Liberation*, trans. and edited by Sister Caridad Inda and John Eagleson. New York: Orbis Books, 1972.

M. Douglas Meeks, *Origins of the Theology of Hope*. Philadelphia: Fortress Press, 1974.

CONCLUSION— STATUS AND PROSPECTS

NICHOLAS PIEDISCALZI

Status of the Dialogue

Several individuals in the West have alleged that the Marxist-Christian dialogue is dead. The foregoing chapters reveal the opposite. The encounter is alive and, in some areas, quite active. To be sure, there are at least two major dialogues, and even though they share several common concerns, they are markedly different. Moreover, even though the First and Second World dialogue continues to exist, it has reached an impasse in Western Europe and the United States and no longer displays the vitality it possessed in the 1960's.

Several events produced this situation. First, the attitudes and policies of the Soviet Union and the United States in the late 1960's and early 1970's created barriers to dialogue. The Soviet Union's reversion to Stalinist practices towards intellectuals made it virtually impossible for them to participate openly and freely in public dialogues. This regression also forced some outstanding leaders to take refuge in Western countries. L. Kolakowski, for example, moved to Great Britain. Furthermore, the Soviet invasion of Czechoslovakia in August of 1968 decimated one of the dialogue's leading centers.

Key leaders in the Czechoslovakian dialogue were forced to flee their homeland. After the Soviet intervention, J. M. Lochmann taught and lectured in the United States before settling in Switzerland. The August invasion also deprived Western Communist parties of some of their leading dialogists, as exemplified by the expulsion of Roger Garaudy from the French Communist party for his condemnation of the Soviet invasion.

The United States' involvement in the Vietnam War created strains in some of its newly opened relations with Communist countries. These strains, in turn, produced barriers to dialogue between Americans and their counterparts in those nations. In addition, the U. S. government's refusal to recognize the demands of many of its own citizens and groups for a cessation of the conflict and its destructive reaction to dissenting groups —for example, police violence during the 1968 Democratic convention in Chicago, the killing of students at Kent State University by National Guardsmen, and the mass arrests in Washington, D. C.—along with setbacks in domestic programs and race relations, created a mood of pessimism which directly and indirectly impeded the advancement of dialogue.

Professor Rosemary Ruether claims that a sense of discouragement pervades the ranks of potential dialogists in the United States due to the fact that "a militaristic madness, destructive of every value, seems to have captured the handles of power."[1] Individuals and groups devoted to reform become more and more powerless. At a growing rate they are withdrawing from action because they find it futile to address "a government that turns a deaf ear, not only to moral outrage, but even to some of the more reasonable kinds of *Real-politik*."[2]

Furthermore, this discouragement is exacerbated by the fact that many Americans believe that our country's serious problems cannot be solved by the existing party system. The major political parties seem incapable of instituting the reforms necessary to solve our basic moral, socio-economic and racial problems. Watergate adds to this despair.

Ruether also points out that many of the changes required in the United States do not engender the "infectious hope" characteristic of the Latin American encounter. Unfortunately, according to her, those who are dedicated to reform in the United States are not able to predict rapid and dramatic advancements as do their Latin American counterparts. Rather, they must utilize counteractive measures, *e.g.*, preventing the President from illegitimately using the power of his office, placing restraints on the military-industrial complex and decentralizing the power of the large corporations. "This is a far less energizing task than liberation. Its watchword is 'resistance,' rather than revolutionary self-expansion. . . ."[3]

Coupled with all of these factors is the reality that the Western dialogue has been limited to elite groups of intellectuals. Hence, since their activities have been curtailed by the policies and actions of the Soviet Union and the United States and the sense of pessimism described by Ruether, it is easy for those who do not look beyond the surface to infer that the Marxist-Christian dialogue is dead. However, those who reach this conclusion overlook the continuing efforts of dialogists such as Aptheker, Ogletree and Lochmann, just to mention three, and ignore the uninterrupted and highly productive encounters in Hungary and Yugoslavia—important members of the First and Second Worlds.[4] Therefore, it is more accurate to say, as we have, that the Western European and American dialogue is at an impasse while the encounters in Hungary and Yugoslavia are advancing.[5]

Moreover, Third World critics who allege that the First and Second World Dialogue is dead also fail to recognize that important leaders in the encounter call for a revitalized and action-oriented encounter. They ignore, for example, that in 1968 both Thomas Ogletree and Paul Lehmann declared that the most important task for the dialogue is to develop a methodology for corrective and reforming action.[6] Both agree with the admonition of the Yugoslavian philosopher Zdenko Roter: "Dialogue that is directed, supervised and limited by an institution can be nothing but a farce, an anti-dialogue."[7]

To describe the two Marxist-Christian dialogues now in existence and to seek to explain in part why one of the encounters has reached an impasse is to deal with only one-half of the problem. It is necessary also to consider the prospects for these dialogues. To this task we now turn.

Prospects for the Dialogue

The Third World Dialogue—despite the recent reversals experienced in Chile—will continue to grow and make advancements. Its leaders will continue to be

105

highly critical of First and Second World Marxists and Christians for failing to deal with mankind's most serious problems. However, their own advancements and reversals eventually will force them to confront some of the same problems now facing the First and Second World dialogists, *viz.*, how to prevent their leadership from becoming rigid and dogmatic; how to maintain their dedication to constant reformation and renewal of policies and programs in the midst of increasing centralization of power and bureaucratization; how to avoid fixating at the technological-industrial stage of development and sustain the motivation and momentum necessary to move beyond the industrial-technological revolution.

On the other hand, the Western European and American dialogue needs to transcend its present impasse. There are two avenues of change which can be followed simultaneously. First, lines of communication and relationships can be strengthened between the dialogists in Western Europe and America and those in Hungary and Yugoslavia. The latter can be of immense help to the former in revitalizing their dialogue through sharing their experiences and new cooperative ventures and offering constructive criticisms.

The adoption of the action-oriented model of the Third World in modified form provides a second means whereby Western dialogists may move beyond their impasse. The editors of this volume in a recent consultation with a leader of the World Council of Churches came to the conclusion that the formation of small study-action groups which would meet in Third World countries and consist of First, Second and Third World participants would be an effective way to help the First and Second World encounter move forward. Such groups should consist of workers, students, academecians and professionals. These groups should devote themselves to helping the participants from each world enrich each other's experiences, determine the meaning of their individual activities, discover their unrecognized problems, and explore strategies for developing programs of co-operative action. These groups also should stress the need for each world to develop its own unique program of action and reform. The emphasis should be on unity, not uniformity. This is necessary because each world confronts unique problems which require unique solutions developed by its own people, rather than pat answers propounded by outside groups. Furthermore, such an emphasis is needed so as to prevent irresponsible and overdramatic criticisms of each other. Such criticisms weaken the sense of unity necessary for strengthening and improving the dialogue. Moreover, Third World Marxists and Christians who criticize severely First and Second World dialogists for not organizing and conducting revolutions in their countries ignore Marx's and Lenin's injunctions against ill-timed revolutions doomed to failure because the conditions and time for their success are neither right nor propitious. They also appear to be unaware that Marx believed that revolutions can be achieved peacefully through the political process.[8]

These groups also should explore ways of transforming the Marxist-Christian dialogue into a world con-

107

gress, perhaps even according to the model of the International Labor Organization whose members come from all nations for the purpose of improving the working conditions of laboring people throughout the world. Such a Marxist-Christian congress could devote itself to seeking, suggesting and implementing solutions to the socio-economic and political problems confronting both the Communist and non-Communist countries. The membership of this congress should include representative spokesmen from government, management, labor and ecclesiastical bodies. These representatives should be selected from both the conservative and reforming elements in these institutions. The vision for this effort already is possessed by leaders in both encounters. Zdenko Roter has summarized their aspirations:

> The common duty of Marxists and Christians is the identification of obstacles and barriers that hinder the affirmation of humanism in the present moment, of those obstacles which extend from differences between rich and poor, from the famine of millions, from militarism, from racial, religious, ideological segregation, from the anti-human effects of technology, from commercialization and from rigid institutionalism of contemporary societies, from domination of capital to bloody wars. The Marxist message of struggle and love and the Christian message of hope and involvement and love cannot be an unidentified and obscure force, but they must lead Marxists as well as Christians into a total involvement in the suppression of the unjust and anti-human social structures.[9]

Any attempt to change the dialogue into a world congress must include China, if it is to be truly interna-